Heaven on Earth

The world's best family holidays

Kids

SARAH SIESE

Beach

Chill and Thrill

Magical Mystery

Safari

Snow

Useful Stuff

DESTINATIONS

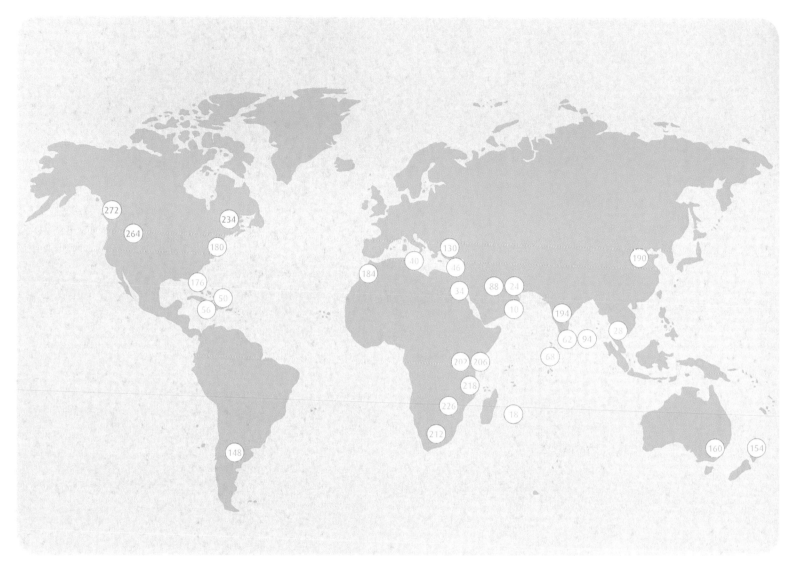

PAGES

Beach

Chill and Thrill

Magical Mystery

Safari

Snow

INTRODUCTION

Taking your children on holiday doesn't have to be two weeks of kiddie-chaos; hours of re-reading the same page of your book, keeping the proverbial 'one eye' on the children while attempting to get some rest and relaxation yourself. We all do enough juggling in our day-to-day lives – holidays should be exempt. But how do you get it right?

The first step is to decide what kind of holiday you're after and work out if the ages of your children match your activity aspirations. There's little point taking a two-year-old on safari, or for that matter, a nine-year-old to visit Father Christmas.

At long last hotels have woken up to the commercial sense of catering for families in a sensitive and sophisticated way and it's now big business. Thankfully, much of the industry has transformed its attitude to children and we are no longer hostage to the holiday camp red-coats of the world when considering a family break.

As adults, we can find ourselves stuck in a rut – with familiar people, places and plans. Children on the other hand see each new dawn as an opportunity to get out and explore. They charge at life optimistically, learning what the world has to offer with open eyes and open hearts, believing anything and everything is possible. They can conquer the world.

Travelling with my own kids is a constant reminder of what it means to live on this planet. There is literally a world of discovery out there, much of which now welcomes children. And seeing it all through their eyes merely enhances the experience. Yes, you have to choose activities carefully and strike the right balance and it's hard getting it spot on every time. But when you do, wow do you know.

Children voted (almost without exception) 'having other children to play with' as top of the list for what's important on holiday, which means that more often than not, family holidays are about spending time with other families. While parents look for a spell of peace and pampering, kids want fun. It can be a tightrope act, balancing everyone's needs and desires or it can flow like the Ganges and be full of spontaneity and thrills. It all boils down to realistic expectations.

Knowing where to go, steering clear of family-phobic hotspots, is half the secret. *Heaven on Earth Kids* is divided into five areas covering different kinds of holidays highlighting various activities, appropriate energy provisos and the optimal age group for each. Tested by parents and offspring, satisfaction for all was the challenge. One thing every holiday featured has in common is the promise of a warm welcome for young guests and enthusiasm with a capital E.

It's worth mentioning that none of the hotels or operators have paid to be included in *Heaven on Earth Kids*. First time mummies tested hotels promising great things for babies; little girls tried the girly stuff while teenagers put the 'teen' activities through their paces. Our young guinea pigs came in all shapes and sizes and tested every club, restaurant and activity, sparing no punches with their feedback. It may be subjective but it's definitely honest.

We live in a time when the world has never been so accessible. Who knows how long it will continue? Sharing it with our children, in my book, is the very nectar of life.

Beach

Sun, sea and sand make the perfect trio and most families chose a beach holiday as their one must-have annual experience. It's the ideal tonic to our long, grey winters. Kids of all ages just love the seashore and whether it's hermit crab racing, building sandcastle empires, sailing, shell collecting, snorkelling or simply sunbathing, the traditional seaside holiday is difficult to beat. The world's favourite family-friendly beach destinations are excellent ambassadors for kids entertainment because they have the help of nature's top ingredients for fun. On the beach it doesn't take much to see them as happy as sandboys.

ARABIAN ADVENTURE

Oman

'Oman must be the new Dubai', I thought looking at their proximity on the map. In reality, I could not have been further from the truth. Yes, they both share the same latitude and climate, both have golden desert-lands and cerulean coastlines but Oman's benefits come with a conspicuous historic culture and sense of place that you just don't encounter in its sister state. Don't get me wrong, I'm a fan of Dubai and salute its achievements, it's just that when it all boils down to it, there's more Varanasi than Vegas in this girl's heart. I like to feel touched by a place on my journeys, as if a small print has been placed indelibly on my memory, from which I can retrieve the tastes and sounds and more importantly the local characters I encountered along the way.

On all counts, Oman represents a treasure trove of experiences for families. Let's get children's priorities straight; swimming does come before souks and henna before history, but with careful planning, a fun balance is easily struck. Oman is sunny, clean, has next to no crime, is exceptionally friendly and over half the population speaks English. The political mantra is education, education, education and my daughter Rosanna was particularly impressed that the State puts its money where its mouth is, giving each secondary school child a hundred dollars a month 'pocket money' to encourage learning. She was all for emigrating.

For millennia water was the Sultanate's most precious commodity, but when oil was discovered in the 1970s, Oman enjoyed new prosperity. Keen to protect its culture, it moved at its own pace, slower than its neighbours, taking time to observe and learn. You could be left unaware of many modernisations; the telephone exchange looks like an old fort; new buildings are built in traditional style and the government has laid over 700 kilometres of pipelines under the sea, to preserve the views. Oil brought the car industry, which in turn meant roads. At the start of his reign there were only ten kilometres of tarmac anywhere in the land; today over 10,000 kilometres of treacle smooth surfaces stretch across the Sultan's nation. And they love him for it. The Sandhurst-trained Sultan Qaboos bin Said is a celebrated and admired leader, respected for the way he has united and guided his people into the twenty-first century.

Strong traditions

Tradition still reigns strong in Omani society. It is commonplace to light frankincense and sprinkle rose

Oman represents a treasure trove of experiences for families

water on the hands of guests in honour of their visit. Men are elegantly dressed in cool flowing white *dishdasha* with scented *furakha* or tassel and intricate filigree-worked silver *khanjar* hanging from the waist – purely for decoration our affable guide Hussain assured. In comparison women are predominantly dressed in black *abayas* and gold or indigo *burkhas* emphasising flamboyant eye make-up, colourful jewellery and diaphanous veils.

In a land made rich on trading there are plenty of shopping opportunities for local produce from each region. Muscat men have long-been recognised for their trading and sailing abilities. From the tenth century, dhows sailed to far reaching shores creating an Omani empire that stretched from exotic Zanzibar to the Afghanistan-Pakistan border, trading in everything from silks and spices, to warriors and slaves. Hussain knew how to hook the children's attention as he engaged them in tales of Sinbad the Sailor and his travels in search of treasure across the globe.

Muscat's a singularly sanitary city where you're fined more for a dirty car than for speeding – the spotless roads are lined with whitewashed villas, manicured municipal gardens and gleaming vehicles that look like they've just driven off a forecourt. Locals are particularly proud of their new mosque. Finished in 2001 and costing more than three hundred million dollars, its cool shiny marble exterior defies the intricate grandiosity that lies within. Home to the largest carpet in the world, an Iranian masterpiece, which took six hundred women three years to weave, not to mention the seven-tonne Swarovski crystal chandelier whose droplets radiate a golden light over the 6,000 all-male congregation Islam is very much alive. Children over ten are allowed in but need to cover their heads with the scarves provided at the entrance.

The colourful Sultan's Palace is flanked by two forts built by the Portuguese in 1587, strategically placed to guard the entrance to the city, also acting as sentinels to the palace. A little further along, Muttrah's fish market is a real eye-opener for children. Packed to the brim with white-robed men touting a 'stinky'

above **The stunning Hajar Mountains**   below **Hide and seek in Jebrin**

array of giant gambas, waist high tuna and eponymous trumpet fish. The nearby souk is good for souvenir shopping and local produce such as pink rose buds, painted perfume bottles of precious frankincense, simple *kunjas* and cotton *dishdasha* (at a mere ten dollars an irresistible buy).

Dramatic and memorable

Muscat now has two luxury family-orientated hotels. The newest is the vast Shangri-La Barr al Jissah Resort, which is really three hotels rolled into one mega-resort. For families the best choice is the Al Waha section with its complex of interconnecting shallow pools where kids can let off steam to their hearts content without upsetting anyone.

Our favourite hotel was a little further down the coast. Arriving at the Al Bustan Palace Hotel at night was dramatic and memorable. Sitting in an oasis between beach and mountains like a knight's sanctuary from marauding Orcs in a *Lord of the Rings* film-set, its opalescent dome, turrets and archways shimmering as searchlights criss-crossed the starry skies. The cavernous lobby could easily host a conference of Ents or giant Trolls. Its spaciousness grew on us as healthy servings of good weather, fine service and aromatic foods ironed out what remained of home pressures. The Chinese restaurant was particularly good and amazingly well set up for children, who decided that Chinese, eaten with chopsticks held together with elastic bands followed by novel fortune cookies, was their new favourite food.

Each day we snorkelled with the resident turtles, and, just as we despaired of seeing dolphins in the bay, we spotted three gracefully dipping and diving only metres from the shore. Al Bustan's scenic beach is great for kids – hundreds of metres of private paradise. You literally walk the red carpet down to the shore, rolled and unrolled each day to save you from scorching your feet.

A two-hour drive from Muscat, through the dramatic Hajar Mountains, lies the fortified town of Nizwa, Oman's old capital. Make sure you go early on a Friday morning, market day, when hectic scenes of cattle and goat trading display locals in full swing. Auction fever is everywhere and, in a shaded corner of the square, we saw feisty bartering over ancient armaments (too precious even for the museum) between proud collectors passionate about national weaponry.

In the vegetable souk, blind men, not privy to eye-medication in the pre-oil days, handled knobbly green pumpkins, huge vats of fresh limes and mountains of coriander and garlic. Interestingly the Bedouin tribes, who spend all day working in the sun, have no eye problems due to the henna-like substance called *Kyhal* they paint on their faces.

After a wander around Nizwa we proceeded through the ruined village of Tanuf to Jabrin, one of hundreds of forts being restored throughout Oman. We wound our way through the lovely town of Bahla and its famous pottery factories stopping to stare at the old fort currently being renovated by UNESCO. In Jabrin we delved into a seventeenth-century castle with wonderful hideaways and painted ceilings. The children found some young Omanis to play hide and seek with, as they chased along the *Falaj*, the ancient irrigation system, which flows through its ramparts.

Aladdin and the Genie's cave

Other overnight trips included four-wheel-drive Wadi bashing, camping under the stars on a hundred-metre-high wave of sand in the Wahiba Dunes in a tent made of goat's hair; swimming in the Wadi Shab – a lush oasis of palm trees, mangos and bananas – and watching turtles hatch under a full moon. The second largest cave in the world has been discovered in Wadi Bani Jabir – the size of seven aircraft hangars – and is said to be the home of the Genie (think Aladdin). Covered in colourful stalactites and stalagmites it's a thrilling sight.

If you're considering an extended stay there's much more to explore. The starkly beautiful Musandam, the northernmost region of Oman, is segregated from the rest the country by the east coast of the UAE (like passing through Canada to reach Alaska). Visitors go to view the Fjords of Arabia at Khor Shamm, which ticks all the boxes along with the surprisingly green pastures of Jebel Harim, Musandam's highest peak.

At the other end of the country, Dhofar's lush greenery, cascades and streams are unique in the Gulf, brought about by the hydrating *Khareef* monsoon. From the first to third centuries, this part of Oman was actually the wealthiest region in the world due to ancient trade in Arabian horses and pure frankincense. Situated on the coast, Salalah's unspoiled beaches are ideal for a plethora of water sports and diving activities. Several luxury family-friendly resorts have opened along the stunning stretch of coast – and dozens more are planning to throw open their doors over the next few years.

So much of Oman is familiar to little ears; tales of Sinbad and Ali Baba, treasure souks, Aladdin and his Genie and the Queen of Sheba. Children watch camels mingle with limousines; spotting satellite dishes on ancient forts and see how the past can live hand in hand with the present.

We concluded that this quiet land is wise to stay clear of pseudo tourism. Its charm lies in its subtle and rather unassumingly gentle way of introducing tourists to its natural wonders and age-old Islamic-cum-Bedouin culture, secure in the fact that once tasted it is never forgotten.

opposite (from top) **Dramatic canyon scenery, four-by-four in the Wahiba Sands, dolphin spotting**
above **Classic rural oasis**

IDEAL AGE: 2–17

For further information contact Oman Tourist Office
Tel +44 (0) 20 8877 4524
www.omantourism.gov.om

INFINITY-EDGED PLAYGROUND

One&Only Le Touessrok, Mauritius

It was once a sleepy island known almost exclusively to French travellers and those interested in the chronicles of the dodo. But in the last ten years Mauritius has conspicuously risen in status to become one of the world's premier playgrounds for the rich and famous, giving the popular Caribbean island of Barbados a good run for its money. What is all the fuss about? Stories of unparalleled service, a coral reef to vie with the Maldives and a collection of some of the world's best family hotels from which to choose certainly make it impossible to ignore.

Mauritius has been ruled by many nations including the Portuguese, Dutch, French and most recently the British from 1810 to 1968, but it was the French who had the greatest influence on the island's culture, language, religion and civil law. Surprisingly the British agreed to maintain what the French had established, which explains why so much of the island feels French but with a distinctively British attitude. The official language is English but French is more frequently used and Creole remains the lingua franca.

The first thing that strikes you as you land on this droplet in the Indian Ocean is the dramatic scenery. Handsome mountain peaks covered in emerald green grasses drop straight into cerulean blue waters – an everyday view from just about anywhere on the island.

Brochures colourfully illustrate dozens of hotels and the groups Beachcomber, Naïade, Oberoi, Accor, Club Med, Constance and Kerzner are all well represented on this pleasure isle. There's the sophisticated Le Saint Géran with its Peter Pan themed thatched clubhouse tucked away between the lagoon and tennis courts; or for children wanting to learn to scuba dive or do an undersea walk I recommend the nearby Le Coco Beach.

In spite of this, one hotel sticks out as particularly impressive for all age groups. Fifty minutes from the airport, Le Touessrok looks like a whitewashed Mediterranean style village. The first, and lasting, impression of Le Touessrok is that it is hugely spacious. Named after an island in Brittany called Tu-Es-Roc ('You Are Rock'), it is divided in two parts: the main resort and a small islet called Frangipani linked by an unusual covered wooden bridge.

Its 193 bedrooms are designer-chic and very contemporary with subtle tropical nuances like carved wooden screens and vibrant Mauritian artwork. Designer Janice Clausen has created something fresh

The first thing that strikes you as you land on this droplet in the Indian Ocean is the dramatic scenery

opposite **Franjipani Island Suite**

for world travellers on the premise that, 'luxury no longer has to be traditional'. Huge bay windows give access to dramatic sea views as the changing light reflects different shades across the horizon. The semi open-plan bathrooms, housing bathtubs that look like sliced eggshells, allow you to wallow in bubbles while staring out to sea. You get the feeling that the design ethic has been fanatical – the result is distinction.

Making your mind up

For epicureans Le Touessrok is a paradise. A dynamic form of gastronomic multiplicity has been created so that you can eat food from all around the globe. Set on three levels, Three-Nine-Eight features nine different cuisines: Mauritian, Indian, Middle-Eastern, Chinese, Thai, Japanese, Spanish, Italian and French all prepared in eight open-plan kitchens. As if that wasn't enough, the resort also has a specialised Michelin level Indian restaurant, Safran, offering a modern interpretation of classical Indian cuisine cooked in its two tandoori ovens, and an Asian-European fusion

restaurant, Barlen's, with stunning views overlooking Trou d'Eau Douce Bay. Making your mind up what to eat has never been more demanding.

Based along a secluded cove overlooking a lagoon and coral reef, the resort's main beach is picture perfect, washing up pretty shells and miniature starfish each morning. A five-minute boat ride takes you to the very private Ilot Mangénie, a little sanctuary that feels like your own romantic desert island. Exclusively reserved for Le Touessrok guests, it's perfect for peaceful daydreaming or a stroll along the deserted beaches in search of shells. The appropriately named Robinson and Friday proved ideal hosts for a barefoot lunch on the beach of fresh dorado and woodfired pizza.

For something more active a wide range of complimentary water sports is available from the resort's private pontoon on nearby Isle aux Cerfs, protecting the tranquillity on the beaches around the hotel. The eighteen-hole par-seventy-two champion golf course, designed by Bernhard Langer, is also located

Huge bay windows give access to dramatic sea views as the changing light reflects different shades across the horizon

on this island surrounded by dramatic sea views and mangrove forests – again just five minutes by boat from the main jetty.

Undaunted instructors

I rate the KidsOnly club at Le Touessrok among the very best in the world. It is often written, but in this case it is true to say, that nothing was too much trouble for the staff at the Robin Hood themed club – we had to entreat our children to spend some time in the 'Mummy and Daddy's club', and found ourselves furtively going to see what they were doing and why they preferred their club to being with us on the beach (a first). Our parental espionage proved to be good spectator sport; hardly believing our eyes as we watched the undaunted instructor patiently teach our four-year-old how to water-ski (all inclusive) on a purpose made ski-cum-boogie-board. The squeals of laughter and joy were all too evident – they were having the time of their lives. Undersea walks, golf, kite flying, crab hunts, glass bottomed boat trips, team games on the beach, sailing races and snorkelling adventures to find hidden treasure. We decided we couldn't compete, sat back and enjoyed some respite.

The Givenchy Spa adds a sophisticated touch to the resort's abundance of leisure options. Decorated with archival sketches and classic designs from the Parisian couturier, its eight therapy rooms offer everything from Lomi-Lomi to the Canyon Love Stone Therapy. If top notch pampering is what you seek, its holistic approach for rebalancing mind and body won't disappoint – a warning: it's so popular you'll need to make your reservations well in advance.

For the children, it was an infinity-edged playground; they would have stayed awake twenty-four hours a day if their energy – and parents – had permitted. For us, Mauritius more than lived up to its build-up – a friendly paradise perfect for relaxation, water sports, golf, fishing and too much good food. The only thing that was missing was the dodo.

One&Only Le Touessrok, Trou d'Eau Douce, Mauritius
Tel + 23 (0) 402 7400
www.oneandonlyresorts.com

193 rooms
Double rooms from €330
The Ocean suites on Frangipani island are the best for families as they can be connected to an adjoining junior suite

KidsOnly club for children aged four to eleven, open daily from 10.00 a.m. – 10.00 p.m.

above **Aerial view**
opposite **Views and children's facilities**

TWENTY-FIRST CENTURY WORLD

Jumeirah Beach Hotel, Dubai

Once a small fishing port, the Gulf Coast emirate of Dubai is now a fascinating fusion of ancient culture and vibrant modernity. Its oil wealth has enabled it to invest in desalination plants, telecommunication systems and all the trappings of technology but, when the oil runs dry, Dubai can fall back on one commodity that will never run out: the sun.

All-year sunshine has made this a popular choice for solar-starved Europeans. Add to this white sandy beaches, superb facilities and excellent service, plus great shopping, golf and racing, and it's easy to see why Dubai has been catapulted into the leading ranks of world-class holiday destinations. The skyline is changing by the week and as the 'Palm' and the 'World' developments take form like giant dot-to-dot pictures. We are literally witnessing the birth of a new civilization. It's a twenty-first century playground for recreation, full of glitz and razzmatazz.

For first time visitors it is an endless surprise. In little more than a generation, this sleepy emirate has transformed itself into a cosmopolitan city – the Vegas of the east. One of its most stunning constructions is the prominent Jumeirah Beach Hotel, known as the Wave, housing 598 sea-facing rooms, suites and villas on twenty-six floors. It has unspoilt beaches, four swimming pools, a magnificent variety of restaurants and sporting facilities, and a terrific kids' club – in fact, of all the top hotels along this coastal strip, the Jumeirah offers the optimum experience for families: of course, there are superb facilities for adults, but children are by no means sidelined.

Elements of nature

Entering the hotel, you're immediately drawn into its 'Elements of Nature' theme. Different floors represent earth, air, fire and water through distinct colour schemes dividing the hotel into four separate levels: restful blues and greens for water; comforting browns and muted reds for earth; tranquil blues and white for air; and brilliant reds and yellows depicting a vibrant sun. Take your pick as the mood takes you.

The theme of nature's elements is carried throughout the bedrooms and corridors, culminating in the Atrium, which features a colossal sculpture ninety metres high, portraying a satellite view of the earth with the United Arab Emirates at its centre, complete with a galaxy of stars and a moon in orbit.

Dining is a serious affair in Dubai and is at the heart of the Jumeirah Beach Hotel, whose twenty restaurants, cafes and bars represent every region of the world.

It's a twenty-first century playground for recreation, full of glitz and razzmatazz

The Apartment restaurant is based on the concept of a 'home away from home' interior of a residential apartment, and includes a bar, music room, cellar and dining room offering a gourmet menu prepared by two-star Michelin chef Patrick Lenotre.

On the twenty-fifth floor La Parrilla is the first and only Argentinean restaurant in the region, where fine steak is cooked before your eyes to a melting tenderness while tango musicians and dancers cavort around the room. Al Khayal is a traditional Lebanese restaurant styled after an Arabic tent. Der Keller reflects the atmosphere of a stylish, rustic German restaurant serving traditional food from different parts of Germany, Switzerland and Austria. Alternatively, choose Carnevale – an authentic Italian restaurant offering traditional pastas.

If you take a trip along the Marina breakwater you reach one of Dubai's most ingenious venues – the circular Seafood Market, elegantly decorated and offering the freshest and finest seafood in the Gulf, displayed on a specially designed ice show table. It's worth trying the innovative Asian fusion menu that combines traditional dishes from Asia with new European cuisine.

Situated on the ground floor of the Pavilion Marina, the Waterfront restaurant allows easy access to the hotel's private beach and marina where children can enjoy time in the sand while parents are having lunch. Between meals there are plenty of options for amusement. The Sports Club overlooking the beaches is a two-storey building situated on the Marina breakwater between the bay and tennis courts. Downstairs it offers many activities including tennis, squash, water sports and a PADI dive centre. Upstairs features a gymnasium with sixty nautilus machines and a free weights section. In addition, the health suite incorporates all the usual water treatments and spa therapies.

Outside there are four swimming pools. The leisure pool, a twenty-five metre training pool, a family pool and a shallow, shaded children's pool ideally located right next door to Sinbad's Kids Club, which has a clubhouse designed like a ship.

The club offers a programme of activities for children under the supervision of highly trained and qualified staff. Children can come and go throughout the day and take part in the daily activity programme, which includes arts and crafts, nature trails and swimming games.

Small children flock to the family adventure playground, consisting of raised walkways with a variety of safety-conscious, padded play features including swings, tunnels and rope walkways. For older children the water sports on offer include sailing, water skiing, parasailing, snorkelling, wind surfing, scuba diving, kayaking, boogie boarding, wake boarding and banana boating.

Fun factory

For all guests, other outdoor facilities include seven floodlit competition standard tennis courts, one of which is multipurpose to include volleyball and basketball, a mini putting green and golf driving nets surrounded by three butler-serviced beaches.

Last but certainly not least, the next-door Wild Wadi Water Park is an attraction as popular with adults as it is with children. For guests of the hotel, entry is free to the twelve acres of themed water activities that includes twenty-three adrenaline-pumping rides that leave you gasping for more.

In a nutshell, the Jumeirah experience is a never-ending kaleidoscope – a fantastic fun factory in the sun for kids of all ages.

Unspoilt beaches, four swimming pools, a magnificent variety of restaurants and sporting facilities, and a terrific kids' club

IDEAL AGE: 4–16

Jumeirah Beach Hotel, PO Box 11416, Dubai, UAE
Tel + 971 4 3480000
www.jumeirahbeachhotel.com

598 rooms
Deluxe rooms from US$300

Sinbad's Kids Club for children aged between two and twelve, open daily 9.00 a.m. – 9.00 p.m.

opposite **Fun and games at Sinbad's Kids Club and Wild Wadi**

FAMILY THAIS

Evason Hua Hin, Thailand

Hua Hin is unlike most other beach resorts in Thailand: far from Bangkok's bright lights and frantic all-night action, it's very much a family holiday destination. As a seaside town it offers the best Thai seafood in the country, served by so many international restaurants that you're spoilt for choice. On top of this, there's tempting shopping, nightly street markets and Thailand's first golf course.

It became popular as a summer retreat in the 1920s after the construction of the railway line from Bangkok. A beautiful colonial-style hotel was built in 1923, and the area finally became well established as a beach resort when King Rama VII built a beach-side palace named 'Klai Kangwon' where the Thai royal family customarily holiday each year.

Intelligent luxury

Three hours south of Bangkok at Pranburi, roughly thirty kilometres south of Hua Hin, you'll find the Evason Hua Hin Resort and Spa. Set among twenty acres of beautifully landscaped tropical gardens filled with lotus ponds and waterways, the resort faces the Gulf of Siam. Designed and operated by Six Senses hotel guru Sonu Shivdasani (of Soneva fame), together with his creative director wife Eva, the hotel was bound to be a success from the outset. Jointly, they have moved away from using all too common old-fashioned stereotypical concepts and have created a mode of what Sonu describes as 'intelligent luxury'. This embraces a 'can do' style and service ethic that is a pleasure for guests and considerate to the local environment and indigenous population.

Eight separate two-storey buildings set among manicured tropical gardens accommodate 145 luxurious guestrooms. There are also forty generous stand-alone villas each with a private pool. A number of interconnecting Evason and Studio rooms have been designed with families in mind and are filled with child-friendly furniture, a box full of toys and various board games for hours of entertainment (a Play-Station is also available on request).

All rooms have twin or king-sized beds covered in 'tropical tog' duvets, and a full-sized day bed that can be used as a sofa during the day. A third bed is available at night on request. Secluded pool villas, shaded by massive banana plants and coconut-laden palm trees, have the added benefits of their own butler, a private plunge pool and a sunken outdoor bathtub surrounded by a lotus pond – bath time has never been more popular. Fun is at the forefront of every mind, and at night

Secluded pool villas, shaded by massive banana plants and coconut-laden palm trees

housekeepers place sand-filled cotton lizards under pillows and bed legs to amuse children.

High-quality dining at affordable prices is a major consideration at Evason, with a number of gourmet options for all tastes. The Restaurant serves a sumptuous buffet breakfast including popular local dishes in a semi al fresco location, to the sound of local musicians playing *kaens*, *suengs* and *ranardaiks*.

The casual open-air Beach Restaurant next to the seashore entertains children with its windowed show kitchen operating a traditional wood-fired pizza oven. It serves gourmet breakfasts to the sound of the ocean's waves, an à la carte lunch menu, and a special seafood menu at dinner that changes daily. Beside the pool a two-level, open-air bar offers a sophisticated snack menu – ideal for kids' lunches at any time of day – and a special gourmet dinner menu.

At night the whole hotel is transformed by hundreds of flickering candles illuminating paths throughout the grounds, lending an atmosphere of sanctuary and calm after a full day with the children. The Other Restaurant specialises in creative Asian fusion cuisine, and opens for dinner in either the chic air-conditioned dining room or al fresco courtyard for those who prefer to dine in the balmy tropical air overlooking terraced lotus ponds.

opposite **'Jungle' walkways**
above **Children's pool**

left **Pool villa**   right **The Restaurant**   oppposite **Beachfront swimming pool**

Roasting marshmallows on the bonfire while singing 'Ging-gang-goolie' under the starlit sky

Evason's holistic Six Senses spa is one of the prettiest in Asia and provides an extensive menu of relaxing and revitalising treatments in the five thatched *salas* each surrounded by tranquil pools. Inside the spa there are six treatment rooms including three especially designed for couples, two dry saunas and two steam rooms – it's definitely a place for expert pampering.

Little VIPs

Facilities for children are exceptionally good. Younger ones are supervised by qualified staff dedicated to providing an exciting list of locally orientated activities including umbrella painting, Thai language lessons, kite flying, beach nature walks, batik printing, junior yoga, soap carving and archery, to name but a few. They're treated like little VIPs at Just Kids!

– the hotel's professionally managed club. Next to the Mr McGregor-style vegetable garden, the club has a canopied swimming pool with bamboo waterspout, adventure playground and a huge activity list ideal for children aged between four and twelve. Real thought has gone into what children will enjoy and, while they're happy just to splash in and out of the pool most of the day, an hour or two of respite in the club is a welcome option for all parties.

Older children are offered such entertainments as elephant trekking, go-karting, tennis and swimming lessons. They can also enjoy the option of a sleepover – pitching their own tents, setting up sleeping bags and roasting marshmallows on the bonfire while singing 'Ging-gang-goolie' under the starlit sky.

It's easy to keep little girls out of the midday sun here. Down on the beach local Thai women cheerfully plait

hair and paint nails under their shady canopies during siesta time. Throughout the day, staff walk around the poolside offering fresh water melon and ice lollies for 'good children' – and adults.

Adults in search of adventure can choose from a lengthy list of unusual activities including tandem sky-diving, a workout around Thanarat's military camp, cave trekking, golf or leisurely sunset cruises.

Evason is an absolute hit for children and adults alike, meeting the needs of both in equal doses. Adults feel neither short-changed by the world-class standards of accommodation, food and spa facilities, nor uncomfortable having their little darlings running around barefoot in lolly-stained clothes chasing lizards. The only problem is that at the end of your stay your children will be utterly reluctant to leave – and so will you.

IDEAL AGE: 1–12

Evason Hua Hin Resort and Spa, 9 Moo 3 Paknampran Beach, Pranburi, Prachuap, Khiri Khan 77200 Thailand
Tel + 66 (0) 32 632 111
www.six-senses.com

145 rooms
40 villas
Evason Studio Rooms from US$130

Just Kids! club for children aged between four and twelve, open 24 hours

RED SEA RIVIERA

Four Seasons Sharm El Sheikh, Egypt

Hailed as the Red Sea Riviera, Sharm El Sheikh is located on the Egyptian coastline at the very tip of the Sinai Desert – a small triangle of land linking Asia to Africa via the famous Suez Canal. It is a land of many biblical references, such as Moses' journey to and from Israel to Egypt. It has an unforgiving landscape of dramatic arid peaks, granite outcrops and dusty dry roads leading to remote sounding destinations inhabited by Bedouin tribes and herds of masticating camels. But it also has the Red Sea – a living aquarium that attracts people from all over the world.

Beyond the call of duty

For a close-to-home spot of winter sun Sharm El Sheikh has become increasingly popular, frequented by prime ministers, royalty and celebrities, all after the attractive combination of warm rays and marine life entertainment. The star on the block that everyone is clambering to visit is indisputably the Four Seasons. The 200-room hotel (including sixty-four family suites) is not so much a resort but a village – an Arabian Eldorado of castellated turrets and bloom-lined borders, cascading down a hillside to the sea below. Accommodation is in one- and two-storey, dome-roofed villas, all complete with balconies over-looking the Red Sea shaded by pretty stripy awnings. The main pool is reached via a twelve-seat tram from the lobby, a joyride for children and adults alike.

It has gained a great reputation for families and rightly so. I thought I'd already seen the full extent of Four Seasons' faultless service when I was in New York; I hadn't. Popping back into the room one morning to collect a forgotten pair of goggles I saw the housekeeper dotingly taking the hair out of the children's hairbrushes – way beyond the call of duty but just another example the lengths the staff go to take care of their guests.

During the school holidays the hotel is almost exclusively a family zone (probably a honeymooner's hell); outside these periods it's a great place for anyone. There are no less than five swimming pools. The Gezira pool has been designed with families in mind – square shaped gazebos housing teak loungers provide necessary shade and were full of slumbering babies and toddlers in a post-lunch haze of soporific contentment. The other pools are also family friendly, with the exception of the spa pool, which is designed for laps and solitude.

I can't think of another hotel that caters so generously for children's meals. A high-quality selection

During the school holidays the hotel is almost exclusively a family zone

The endless round of sorbets, watermelon, lollies, and yoghurt smoothies are great bribe-fodder for good behaviour

of freshly prepared foods are displayed on knee-high buffet tables each lunchtime and offered complimentary to any child under twelve. And the endless round of sorbets, watermelon, lollies, and yoghurt smoothies are great bribe-fodder for good behaviour. The kids' menu also reflects careful consideration with Baby Bear's 'just right' porridge, Mama's chocolate pudding and teatime treats of milk and cookies left in your room. Of course, the adult fare is just as delicious. Arabian night at the open-air terrace of the Arabesque restaurant is well worth attending – a selection of Mediterranean, Moroccan and Lebanese specialities are served while children line up for henna tattoos and lessons in flatbread making.

On the pampering front, the Daniela Steiner beauty spa specialises in all-natural cleansing, healing and age-defying beauty treatments. You can opt for either indoor or outdoor treatment rooms complete with saunas and whirlpools.

Many tour guides offer day trips further afield to glimpse the wonders of Luxor, the Nile, and the Pyramids but these are really best left to another trip or add on an extra week when you can do justice to their magnificence. There's plenty to explore around the Sinai.

Biblical wonders

The three-hour car journey from Sharm El Sheikh to the isolated Saint Catherine's Monastery is at once dramatic, and mesmerisingly repetitive. Mile upon mile of rugged terrain, soaked by the year-round sun feels almost like a lunar-land of barrenness. The Greek Orthodox chapel dates back to the forth century when Helena (a Byzantine empress) built it next to the Burning Bush. Two centuries later Emperor Justinian added a fortified monastery to protect the chapel from marauding Bedouins. Soon after that a mosque was added inside the same walls, to safeguard the chapel from passing Arab armies. Its remoteness may have much to do with the fact that so many of its remarkable mosaics, intricately gilded icons and rare manuscripts have been preserved to this day. Some are on display to tourists, who, unfortunately get herded around somewhat

opposite **The family pool**

unceremoniously but can always queue to re-enter for a second glance.

The monastery stands in the shadow of another biblical wonder, Mount Sinai, where Moses received the Ten Commandments. Hiking up to the summit of 2,285 metres is no mean task in the midday sun (the phrase 'only mad dogs and Englishmen' frequently came to mind) but such is its popularity with the faithful of more than one religion that the peak is often crowded before dawn by those coming from around the world to watch the sun rise across the Sinai Desert.

For something rather less energetic, the peninsula of Ras Mohamed, located at the southernmost tip of the Sinai, about twenty kilometres from the hotel, has been a national park since 1983. It extends over 480 square kilometres and includes the islands of Tiran and Sanafir as well as the protected coral reef, coastal dunes and mangrove swamps around Sharm El Sheikh. Swimming and offshore snorkelling trips are very popular as the vibrant coral formations and marine life have made it a premier destination for scuba enthusiasts. The colours, both above and below the clear blue waters, almost defy belief.

left **Steps on Mount Sinai**
below left **Red Sea wonders**
opposite **Four Seasons' beach**

Four Seasons, 1 Four Seasons Boulevard, PO Box 203, Sharm El Sheikh, South Sinai, Egypt
Tel + 20 (69) 360 3555
www.fourseasons.com/sharmelsheikh

136 rooms, 64 suites
Premier Rooms from US$360

Kids For All Seasons club for children aged between five and twelve, open daily 9.00 a.m. – 5.00 p.m.

FAMILY CHIC
The Anassa, Cyprus

Situated on the doorstep of three continents, Cyprus's very location guarantees its visitors exposure to an enchanting blend of history, culture and religion. It's fêted by holidaymakers for its friendliness and warm hospitality and unless you're determined to spend every minute on the beach you'll inevitably stumble across at least one of its other attractions. Archaeological treasures, Byzantine churches, remote monasteries, olive groves, rugged hills and dramatic coastlines all come in plentiful quantities.

It's also an island of strikingly varied terrain, where you can travel from cool pine-clad mountain paths at 2,000 metres to a stifling 40°C on the shores of the Mediterranean Sea in under an hour. Few people realise that you can even ski here in winter.

To be honest, I was quite disappointed by many of Cyprus's hotels (many are a 1970s hangover of the first wave of 'one size fits all' tourism), that was, until I visited the family owned Thanos group of hotels, which include the famous Annabelle, trendy Almyra and the impossible to ignore flagship property, the Anassa.

Situated in grand isolation in the far north-west corner of the island, the Anassa has found an unspoiled spot next to the little fishing village of Polis – where the air is notably cooler and the sea is delectably warmer.

Thankfully, the landscape remains unblemished by unsightly buildings (which blot so many of the southern horizons); instead the rich soil is furrowed with vigorous olive groves and appetising orchards of sweet-smelling oranges and apricots.

The hotel caused quite a sensation when it was built in 1998. Its combination of traditional whitewashed villas and terracotta-tiled roofs has been carefully constructed to recreate a pretty Greek village. There's even a peaceful Byzantine-style chapel and traditional village square surrounded by banks of lavender and bougainvillaea. It's a welcome sight for sore eyes.

Bedrooms are cool, cream, airy and very restful. They possess that solid feeling of stillness normally associated with age-old, thick-walled villas. Some suites even have their own plunge pool or outdoor whirlpool. All have a private terrace facing the western sky from where the early morning scents of jasmine and citrus greet you, combined with eruptions of perfume from the ubiquitous banks of lemon-scented geraniums.

Just around the corner are the baths of Aphrodite, from where this goddess of beauty, love and laughter was spotted emerging from a foaming sea. First thing in the morning, the sea looks like a giant mirror

The rich soil is furrowed with vigorous olive groves and appetising orchards of sweet-smelling oranges and apricots

reflecting an occasional cloud, by midday small white horses appear and rippling waves wash over the beach's myriad multi-coloured pebbles turning the shore it into a gemstone treasure trove. If you're restless, water-sports abound including sailing, para-gliding, scuba and waterskiing. If you want to chill, head for the Romanesque health spa for a mêlée of meditation, aerobics and yoga or a wide menu of Thalasa treatments.

While older children enjoy the sportive opportunities, younger ones (from four to eleven) can be nurtured in the Smiling Dolphins Kiddies Club, which offers a wide array of activities from biscuit making to beach games.

Four exceptional restaurants are supplied with fresh ingredients from Anassa's very own farm, while local fishermen from Latchi promise to provide the daily catch. A simple Greek salad of olives, tomatoes, cucumbers, feta and chopped cabbage dressed in virgin olive oil may be all you feel like in the sweltering midday heat. Come dinner-time don't just stick to the *moussaka*, try the delicious *loukanika* (coriander seasoned sausages) or the traditional *koupepia* (stuffed vine leaves). Dinner may be best enjoyed sitting under the twisted knotted branches of the ancient olive trees watching the Plough cross the sky from east to west. As your meal progresses from course to course, the stars gradually disappear behind the mountain.

The House of Dionysus

Only forty-five minutes away, lies the bustling hub of Paphos port, the island's capital for over 800 years (from the fourth century BC to the fourth century AD), whose population has swelled from a modest 5,000 in the late 1960s to nearly 50,000 today, making it the fourth largest town in Cyprus. Its rapid growth was no fluke. In 1962 a farmer, while ploughing the soil for his potato crop, discovered one of the island's greatest treasures, the House of Dionysus – which includes 600 square metres of Roman mosaics. The delightfully preserved floors depict an abundance of ancient symbols laid out under a single roof. They are simply too rare and too impressive to miss.

right **Hallway and Presidential suite**
opposite **Troodos lace-maker**

To find a taste of the real Cyprus, head inland towards the generous views provided from the summits of the Troodos range. The arid plains that hug the coastline rapidly fall away as you scale the untouched, pine-filled mountains that dominate the heart of the isle. Huge flocks of sheep are herded by Zorba-like fellows astride donkeys draped in colourful blankets. High up in the hills lies the sleepy village of Omodos with its exquisite beamed church and icon-crusted altar. In the cloister, black-stockinged widows sit in the shaded doorways exchanging gossip, industriously working on intricate lace rosettes sold for a pound, while distinguished looking Greek Orthodox priests stroll around the square nodding to visitors.

Most of the Troodos villages appear half derelict; full of tumbledown buildings with decrepit doors hanging on rusty hinges (one knock and they'd disintegrate); yards full of discarded boulders, flower pots, and piles of junk covered by overgrown vines… but they aren't forsaken. Many are still home to families that have lived there for generations. Further down the cobbled lanes at the village café you'll spot the 'old boys' balanced on rickety wooden and straw chairs, playing serious card-games at tables reserved for the village patriarchs. It's the same wonderful sight from village to village.

All around Cyprus you'll find curious notices requesting you not to cross your legs – to cross your legs and arms at the same time is the sign of death and you may be asked to leave.

Inhabited since Neolithic times – in a spectacular position overlooking the sea – the area of Kourion hosts many impressive ruins. The fifth-century house of Eustolios still holds a beautiful inscription,

Enter to thy good fortune
And may thy coming
Bless this house

Lying adjacent, the restored amphitheatre seats 2,500 people and is regularly used by performers who relish its perfect acoustics.

Whatever you choose to do in Cyprus, make sure you leave the beach for a day or two to explore its wealth of beauty and history and remember, if you want to come back, then don't cross your legs.

above **Paphos catacomb**
opposite **Anassa views**

IDEAL AGE: 4–16

Anassa, PO Box 66006, 8830 Polis, Cyprus
Tel + 357 26 888000
www.thanoshotels.com

177 rooms
Garden View rooms from £230
Interconnecting rooms available

Smiling Dolpins Kiddies Club for children aged four to eleven, open daily from 9.00 a.m. – 5.30 p.m. (April to October and during the Christmas holidays)

BABY-GOES-TOO

The Almyra, Cyprus

Good baby-friendly hotels are rarer than hen's teeth. While many now cater to some degree for children aged four and upwards, nowhere is more geared up for babies and toddlers than Cyprus's trendy Almyra hotel. Thought of as the Anassa's younger, hipper sister, the Almyra is Europe's most sticky-finger-friendly, all-crawling-all-dancing, little-miss-molly-coddle designer hotel. And, unlike its big sister, it's affordably chic.

The irony of travelling with tiny-tots is the huge amount of paraphernalia that accompanies you. By the time you've squeezed in all the necessary tot-equipment your baggage allowance is reduced to a crumpled bikini. Almyra's Baby-Go-Lightly has come to the rescue. The idea behind the concept is to order your essential baby-clobber on-line and have it delivered to the hotel free-of-charge in time for your arrival. This way you might even enjoy the journey as you will travel leaner, lighter and happier.

A tick-list of literally everything you could need has been compiled – from car seats for taxis or rentals to story books, puzzles, potties, changing mats, baby bathtubs, buggies, swimming nappies, baby gyms, bouncy chairs, bottles and teats. You really can leave it all at home for once.

Set in eight acres of landscaped gardens on Cyprus's south-west coast, the hotel enjoys uninterrupted views across the bay towards the medieval castle and Paphos harbour. Originally the Paphos Beach Hotel, it has been relaunched as the Almyra meaning 'taste of the sea'. Its success lies in its contemporary style and comfort, catering for family needs.

The 190 rooms are simple, practical and understated. Beds are dressed in pretty baby-blue linen, covered in one-tog white quilted duvets. The designer must have looked out of the window to choose the colours as they perfectly reflect the shades of the sky, sea and stone pier. I particularly liked the more spacious Kyma (meaning 'waves' in Greek) suites down near the beach – they can comfortably accommodate two adults, a child and an infant in a baby cot. There are some interconnecting rooms but they are so popular they need to be booked well in advance.

On the food front the kitchen will happily prepare vegetable compotes and fresh fruit purees, promising quality ingredients and absolutely no additives. Fussy eaters pose a challenge rather than a problem. Thankfully parents don't have to eat mushy peas – Mediterranean specialities and the ever-changing catch of the day are prepared by ex-Nobu chef Rob Shipman.

The hotel enjoys uninterrupted views across the bay towards the medieval castle and Paphos harbour

An expert in flavour-buddies (chocolate and orange, for example), he combines his passion for the purity of Japanese cuisine and sensuality of Mediterranean tastes with great aplomb.

Jasmine and wild thyme

Children are welcome to join the morning and afternoon activity programmes at the Smiling Dolphins Kiddies Club next to the Mosaics Restaurant – open from April to October and during the Christmas holidays. It offers a well thought out programme of activities including nature walks collecting things from the beach to make a giant collage, shows put on by the children with their own hand-made puppets, popcorn jewellery making, face painting, kite design and flying and various team games.

Almyra has two freshwater swimming pools, one designed specifically for children and shaded by billowing awnings. There's a qualified swimming instructor for all ages, English-speaking nannies and sporting activities galore available from the pier.

No baby zone is going to be noiseless. But it's surprisingly calm around the pool and play areas. It's also pushchair distance from all the action in Paphos – Cyprus's answer to St Tropez. But if the touristy neon lights, diamond-filled windows and fast-fish restaurants of the bustling coastal town all get too much, escape to the interior for a dose of solitude. You can get a taste of typical Cypriot life or savour the world's oldest wines. You can smell the jasmine and wild thyme, walk through pine scented forests or you could just chill-out.

opposite **Main pool**   above **Sea view**   below **Balcony room**

IDEAL AGE: 0–12

Almyra, PO Box 60136, 8125 Paphos, Cyprus
Tel + 357 26 888 700
www.thanoshotels.com

190 rooms
Rooms from £120
Limited interconnecting rooms available

Smiling Dolphins Kiddies Club for children aged four to eleven, open daily
9.00 a.m. – 5.30 p.m. (April to October and during the Christmas holidays)

ISLAND HOPPING

The Caribbean

The Caribbean was traditionally considered a romantic escape destination for couples only. Recent years, however, have seen both the quantity and quality of family friendly options fly off the scale. It's no longer an adult-only domain. The islands offering the best facilities tend to be those with direct air access, namely Barbados and Antigua, but if you're happy to take a secondary flight the rewards can be great. What's interesting about the Caribbean is that each island has its own distinct footprint; different terrain, crops, language, food, even architecture varies from island to island. Once hooked you'll be torn between revisiting what you know and love and exploring new options. Whatever the case, the Caribbean offers a giant playground for kids of all ages.

Barbados

The most developed of all the islands, Barbados has a good variety of beaches, with a string of excellent hotels along the fashionable west coast and is the most popular choice for first-time visits to the Caribbean. Indeed many love it so much they never 'risk' trying anywhere else. The south coast has a younger more active stance, while the east remains rugged and wild.

Top of the list and by far the most chi-chi of the west coast's great institutions is the legendary Sandy Lane. Once a house party hideaway, it has had the mother of all makeovers and taken a metamorphic leap to become a super-resort, pretty much in a league of its own. Undoubtedly the most successful hotel in the Caribbean, it pampers its little guests in the knowledge that they are tomorrow's big guests. The Disneyesque Treehouse Club offers an array of supervised activities for pre-teens including arts and crafts and swimming games. Ritzy glitzy gismos and cool decor attract teenagers to the Den, a hangout zone for kids too blasé to hit a ball round the three championship golf courses with their dads while yummy mummies are mollycoddled in the spa.

No less popular and a little further up the coast, traditional style and loyal guests give the family-run Coral Reef a sort of sophisticated clubby feeling (that, some argue, has been forgone by its uptown neighbour). The white wooden cottage suites are particularly well suited to families – scattered around the twelve acres of grounds overlooking lawns and tropical gardens, most with private plunge pools and verandas. Complimentary entertainment for children includes water sports, a tennis pro-clinic,

The Caribbean offers a giant playground for kids of all ages

playground, crèche facilities and two swimming pools. Children tend to wander around in little groups choosing whether to swim, play or just chill out under one of the giant palm trees with the O'Hara grandchildren.

Antigua

Antigua's glut of beaches and low humidity make it an ideal location for family based holidays, and many of the bays and coves have particularly calm and shallow waters perfect for paddling and snorkelling. The south is unspoilt and peaceful – a pastoral scene of goats being herded by a solitary figure strolling towards the ruined sugar mill on a hilly promontory or a man straddling a tame donkey – still a regular sight and popular mode of transport. For those with vivid imaginations, the Pirates of the Caribbean can be re-lived at Nelson's Dockyard where you can wander around the fortifications next to the marina. Our children enjoyed some interactive knot tying, rope climbing and model making in the museum before sailing out on a tropical kayak adventure to swim with the rays at Stingray City.

Carlisle Bay is the hotel that put the Caribbean back on the map after a downturn in the 1990s. Set in its own natural bay on Antigua's southern coast it is in the vanguard of contemporary stylishness. It's a tribute to

opposite **Coral Reef**
above **Sandy Lane**
below **Curtain Bluff**

owner Gordon Campbell Gray that the mucky-mits brigade is allowed anywhere near this metro meets minors haven. Movies are shown everyday in the I'm-a-famous-Hollywood-director-style cinema, which can comfortably seat forty-five children while parents eat their dinner in peace. In fact it's been such a hit with families that Powder Byrne are now running the year-round kids' club.

Just around the bay is the forty-year-old Curtain Bluff – Antigua's veteran when it comes to family fun. A spontaneous programme of 'whatever the kids want to do' is laid on in an apparently seamless fashion. At one point, we had daughters one, two and three, learning to dive for sea biscuits and conch shells, race a catamaran and crab race simultaneously, thanks to the very accommodating and undaunted staff. We lay on the beach exhausted at the thought, overlooking Montserrat's (nicknamed Monster Rat by the kids) smouldering volcanic mass towards the distant silhouettes of Guadalupe and St Kitts. Curtain Bluff may still have swirly-print bedspreads and Florida-cum-Eastbourne decor but its two strikingly different beaches, consummate local staff and relaxed atmosphere make it a winner for families.

All in all the Caribbean is on the up and once you've got your toes in the water, go on and take that extra flight. Try the unhurried pace of Nevis with its old West Indian airs and graces and stay in one of the exemplary Four Seasons villas. Or pop up to the sophisticated British Virgin Islands and marvel at the sweeping crescent of white sand and commendable kids' club at Little Dix on Virgin Gorda. Once you start you won't stop hopping.

above **Carlisle Bay**
opposite **A playground for kids of all ages**

IDEAL AGE: 2 - 16

Island hopping tours can be booked through
www.holidaysfromheaven.com
Tel +44 (0) 118 933 3777

PINEAPPLE PERFECTION

Round Hill, Jamaica

It was with a certain amount of trepidation that I booked my trip to Jamaica but my worries about safety were totally unfounded. It appears that we've been swamped with misinformation – the island and its people are a showcase for the Caribbean at its best.

Our first tastes of Round Hill were delicious. Blissful tranquillity, twenty-first-century comfort and luxury without pretension, combined with privacy and that precious commodity, peace. Well, that was until my entourage of daughters arrived on the beach. Squeals of excitement and laughter ensued as the warm Caribbean Sea licked their ankles. They couldn't wait to go snorkelling with the baby rays, kayaking over the reef or have a bounce on the giant water trampoline.

Lord Monson's century-old sugar and pineapple plantation was transformed in 1953 by the illustrious John Pringle into a haven for the rich and famous, and what a delightful spot in which to build a hotel. The hundred-acre peninsula of lush Jamaican countryside encompasses twenty-seven villas and thirty-six beachside suites in a whitewashed building appropriately named Pineapple House set in a moon shaped bay overlooking crystal clear water. To this day the hotel has retained its clubby atmosphere and

guests still greet each other, welcome newcomers and regularly join tables at mealtimes.

Managing Director Josef Forstmayr modestly confesses to tempting away Sandy Lane chef, Trevor Duncan, but his sin is easily forgiven by guests who enjoy delicious meals al fresco – either by the pool or on the restaurant veranda. Adult fare includes a delectable choice of local and international dishes, a fresh daily catch of local fish, and an irresistible selection of fruit sorbets and deserts. Consistent high standards extend to the kids' menu where children are treated to fresh gougons of chicken or fish, pasta and crudités. And with all the swimming and castle building there's a satisfying spread of clean plates all round.

Some guests make an effort to dress for dinner and there's a certain theatrical bent to evenings as the cocktail hour gets underway and the pianist performs an eclectic repertoire of classical, Disney and Bob Marley songs. There's no doubt that Jamaica's golden era was the 1950s. Ghosts of glamorous gatherings live on in the black and white photographs capturing Round Hill's most celebrated guests and moments. No one's allowed to take themselves too seriously though and oil portraits of dignitaries with pineapple heads highlight Jamaican humour.

Twenty-first-century comfort and luxury without pretension, combined with privacy and peace

above **Grass weaving lessons with a local Rastafarian**   opposite **Pineapple House Suites and views**

Grass weaving
taught by a local
Rastafarian
and myriad
arts and crafts
abound

Pineapple House has been refurbished by Round Hill villa owner, Ralph Lauren. The ocean-fronted bedrooms have brilliant white ceilings, walls and upholstery with an occasional dash of strong colour such as a fuchsia pink sarong or a scattering of royal-blue cushions. Comfy mahogany-stained bamboo four-posters are draped in white toile and dressed in 300-count linen sheets. The white bathrooms are also spacious with huge oblong baths, walk-in showers, double vanities, and yummy local soaps and balms including pure aloe vera. What you'll love best though,

is the view through the broad jalousie windows, across the banana and palm tree fronds to the distant headland. Most dusks provide spectacular sunsets when a hazy swollen sun melts into the sea.

Personal imprint

For something even more luxurious, private and spacious you could rent one of Round Hill's privately owned villas. Nearly all have their own swimming pool and come with personal maid service and in-house meals prepared in your own kitchen. Glowingly elegant,

decorated by the world's most renowned designers, these properties posses the personal imprint of generations of owners who have stamped an enticing home-away-from-home comfort. Their provenance is undeniably impressive; yesteryear's owners were the likes of Noel Coward, the Hammersteins, Rothermeres and Astaires.

Surly service has long been my bugbear of the Caribbean. Not so here. The service is so good you don't even notice it. Staff are copious, present, cheerful and helpful. It all comes down to one man, the ever-present Josef Forstmayr, who has been looking after his staff and overseeing the minutiae for the past fifteen years. The good news is he's here to stay. You'll see him walking around, taking personal interest in his guests' needs; constantly chatting, introducing and dream-fixing – never has a manager been so hands-on.

The excellently run Pineapple Kids' Club, open seven days a week from nine until five o'clock, is complimentary for children aged between three and twelve. Tennis clinics, nature walks, reggae lessons, grass weaving taught by a local Rastafarian and myriad arts and crafts abound. Each day has a different theme: T-shirt and rock painting; nature and treasure hunts; beach Olympics and shell hunting; environment, science and paper craft; followed by an assortment of outdoor games, glass-bottomed boat rides, dancing, drama and cultural programmes. You can rest assured that even when the children aren't with you they'll be getting a true taste of Caribbean culture.

If you book the family suite an additional five hours of nanny-service is there whenever you want it. Thankfully, the proximity of the amenities means that older children are safe to wander between the rooms, beach, pool and kids' club at their will.

Getting out and about

Many spend a whole week lazing by the cascading infinity-edged pool, waiting for a visit from one of the bay's resident dolphins, or being pampered in the spa, which is housed in a handsome Jamaican Great House, but there's plenty to explore outside the hotel.

Some fifty minutes from Round Hill, the Mayfield falls and mineral springs cascade down the hillside forming natural pools and Jacuzzis. They're one of the least known but most picturesque waterscapes

Jamaica has to offer. The trip can be easily combined with lunch at Cosmos on Negril's seven-mile stretch of sand followed by tea at Rick's café where fearless athletes perform acrobatics over the cliffs before diving fifty feet into the cerulean blue sea below.

Swimming with dolphins in Ocho Rios and riding bareback through the surf are favourites with children; as is the spectacular canopy tour, zip-wiring a thousand feet over the jungle roof. Tubing through the rapids or gently rafting along the Great River taking in the plant and bird life offer an unspoilt insight into the island's abundant beauty. Or for something a little more sedate a tour round the eighteenth-century Greenwood and Rose Hall Great Houses. There's plenty to choose to suit all ages and abilities.

The longer you stay the more special it becomes. I've become Jamaica's number one fan – well number four actually, after my three daughters who loved it even more.

right **Private villa pool and pontoon**

IDEAL AGE: 0–16

Round Hill Hotel and Villas, PO Box 64, Montego Bay, Jamaica, West Indies
Tel + 1 (876) 956 7050
www.roundhilljamaica.com

36 rooms, 27 private villas with pools
Pineapple House rooms from US$350

Pineapple Kids' Club for children aged three to twelve, open daily 9.00 a.m. – 5.00 p.m.
Kids tennis clinic available in July and August

THE IRRESISTIBLE ISLAND

The Fortress, Sri Lanka

Sri Lanka is a crazy country but I love it. The island is caught in the classic paradox of where there's good there's bad. Despite the politically charged war that has raged in the north-east for thirty years, the rest of the island sees Singhalese, Tamils and Christians living and working together in harmony. And this provides Sri Lanka with an atmosphere of calm – just one of the teardrop-shaped island's many charms.

For a country the size of mainland Britain its biodiversity is extraordinary with tropical jungle, rainforest, wild game reserves, spectacular mountain ranges and perfect surf beaches all part of the landscape. You will see extreme poverty but you will also see an abundance of vegetation, flowers, fruits and vegetables, which ensure that even the poorest people have enough to eat.

Without question, Sri Lanka is seductive to travellers. Its unique combination of history and culture, charm and romance keeps people coming back. In fact in recent years more and more visitors have ended up extending their stay. Even the tsunami didn't put people off. Many volunteers, who originally headed down to the south coast to help, ended up staying longer and some have still not left, having bought land and adapted to the easy lifestyle.

The area around Galle is particularly beautiful. Galle itself, based around a Dutch fort – now World Heritage Site – is a wonderful old town full of cobbled streets, period houses, local characters and fun little boutiques. You can take an evening promenade around the ramparts with local families who watch boys throw themselves off the walls into the ocean while the sun sinks below the horizon.

Meet the dinosaurs

Heading further south prepare to discover some of the most ideal beaches you have ever seen, perfect for long walks passing only the odd stilt fisherman or hermit crab. Or pop into little beach bars serving simple and delicious fresh seafood and sundown cocktails. Just a little further along the coast Kogolla, famous for its fabulous lake, is so quiet you can revel in the beauty and peace afforded by miles of personal space. Take a small boat and explore the waters, visiting spice and herb gardens, local cinnamon farmers or a little island on which stands nothing but an ancient temple with painted murals. Be ready to meet the dinosaurs – the giant monitor lizards that are actually harmless despite their prehistoric appearance.

Prepare to discover the most ideal beaches you have ever seen

A wonderfully
informal
and friendly
atmosphere
perfect for
families

**The Fortress Hotel views
and interiors**

Kogolla lake is also used for seaplanes, particularly for people flying to and from Colombo who prefer to avoid the three-hour drive, making it the perfect location for the Fortress hotel. A most welcome addition to the Galle area providing all the swankiness and creature comforts you could wish for on a holiday, but with a wonderfully informal and friendly atmosphere perfect for families.

Entering through the impressive Fortress doors makes you feel that you are going into another world. The great portal beckons you on to the fabulous inner courtyard, which comprises a big jungle-like garden leading to a swimming pool area, actually two pools joined together with a bubbling Jacuzzi. The rooms are all funky, fun with sassy modern furniture and very comfortable, kitted out with a plasma TV, DVD player and iPods that can be personally programmed on request; some rooms even have private indoor plunge pools.

If you're checking in with little ones, your room will automatically be furnished with amenities like cots, bath products and cute mini towelling robes. There's also a nursery room with cots, changing tables and on-tap babysitting.

For active kids there's loads to do. The Little Adventurers Club has a lovely playroom equipped

with lots of games, DVDs and a PlayStation. The zone is supervised by an English-speaking member of staff who organises games and daily competitions. The great kids' menu even includes a movie option with film, popcorn and homemade Toblerone – it's available any time and delivered to your room. For older children yoga classes are held three times a week and there are kids' spa treatments offering massages and mother and daughter manicures and pedicures.

For grown ups there are yoga and fitness classes, cultural events and tea tasting. Best of all are the pampering Per Aquum spa experiences – probably the best in Sri Lanka, offering a global menu of international and indigenous ayurvedic therapies.

Icing on the cake

Outside the hotel activities include visits to the turtle hatchery where your kids can wait for a moonlit night to release a baby turtle into the ocean, cricket on the green, trips to the local Wickremasinghe Cultural Museum, picnics in the museum gardens, boat trips on the lake and tuk-tuk rides around Galle Fort. You could even borrow ten-speed mountain bikes to explore the local villages set in vibrant green paddy fields.

Just a little further along the coast, Welligama Bay is one of Sri Lanka's great surfing beaches with plenty of outlets for board rentals. Head further down the coast and you pass more great beaches in Mirissa, Talalla and Tangalle. Carry on and you get to Yala National Park, famous for short jeep safaris, spotting elephants, crocodiles, bears and leopards.

The icing on the cake though will always be the miles of unspoilt beaches wrapping around the south coast, almost empty of tourists, and making Sri Lanka one of the last remaining paradises of South Asia.

opposite **Inland scenery**
right **The Pinawella elephant orphanage**

IDEAL AGE: 4-16

The Fortress
PO Box 126
Galle
Sri Lanka
tel +94 91 4380909
www.thefortress.lk

Fortress rooms from US$510, half board

Little Adventurers Club for children
aged three to twelve, open daily
9.00 a.m. – 5.00 p.m.

HAPPY AS A SANDBOY

One&Only Reethi Rah, The Maldives

At last count, the Maldives had 1,900 islands, 200 inhabited by locals and about a hundred colonized for the sole activity of holidaying. It's an approximate figure because in recent years new resorts have been popping like peas. We're all agreed they look like a honeymooner's paradise but just how suitable is such a tranquil clime for your brood, however well behaved? Well, in truth the majority of islands are best left as an exclusive domain for cooing couples and if children are not explicitly solicited then the general rule is don't go where you're unwelcome.

That said there are a handful of islands that are perfect for families. The phrase 'as happy as a sandboy' couldn't be more fitting for children visiting the Maldives; in essence a giant sandpit surrounded by an irresistibly warm aquarium full of cartoon coloured fish with funny names like *oriental sweetlips*. There's no malaria or vaccinations required and people are as friendly as they come.

The larger islands best suit children's needs for practical as well as esoteric reasons. Space to accommodate an activities club and water-sports in one corner without destroying the sanctuary of peace and quiet for other guests is key to success. Top of the list for older kids and teens is One&Only's flagship Reethi

Rah (literally meaning 'beautiful island') lying only an hour by boat from Malé International airport (with direct flights from Europe, the Middle East and the Far East). It's the largest leisure island in the Maldives – in fact, half-natural and half-fabricated in the shape of a seahorse with over six kilometres of beach.

The 130 villas, many with private pool, are sleek and spectacularly spacious, spread out around the circumference of the island, each with a garden area and ocean view. The offshore breeze that blows three sheets to the wind means that noise doesn't travel further than you, or your neighbours, want it to and makes the need for air-conditioning redundant both day and night. You can choose how to get around: on foot, bicycle, or by electric buggy. And before you can say ahhh, the children will be shell seeking along the shore, a mere seven metres away.

A kid in tow doesn't mean compromise. You'll be met by a guest attendant and welcomed with iced tea cocktails and a soothing ESPA foot massage before a quick orientation of the room and resort, which offers a simpatico blend of comfort and nature, with, I confess, rather more comfort than nature. However, when colours that look like they've been picked out of Aladdin's paintbox surround you, creating an

The 130 villas, are sleek and spectacularly spacious, spread out around the circumference of the island

Reethi Rah main pool and water villas

implausible cocktail of blues and yellows, even Mother Nature seems illusory.

The 'magic' restaurant

Of the three restaurants, our favourite was the higgledy-piggledy *Fanditha* (meaning 'magic'), resembling a ramshackle open-air furniture sale – as if a ship has been wrecked on the reef and all the islanders have rushed to rescue its booty and brought it ashore. Lamps, rugs, hardwood tables and intricately carved treasure chests laid here, there and everywhere. There's something remote and out-of-place about a dining table sitting in bare sand, epitomising the whole twenty-first century trend for barefoot-luxury. It's certainly eccentric and a welcome bolt from the mundane normality of samey restaurants. An added bonus is that teenagers think it's cool too.

As the competition stakes hot up for who can out-do who, hotels are showcasing their innovative service-par-excellence with new fads and fashions. One new ploy to wow guests – and an absolute winner with kids – is personal iPods down on the beach, pre-loaded with over a thousand tracks.

The KidsOnly Club has been designed to give mums and dads some time out while children enjoy non-stop fun with their peers. Located on the south-eastern tip of the island and surrounded by a sand-filled shaded playground, shallow swimming pool, beach and lagoon, the air-conditioned playhouse offers everything from art decks to PlayStations. Understandably most kids just want to be outside, so days are planned with this in mind. A common passion for hermit crab hunting and racing, fish feeding, snorkelling, building sandcastles and crab kingdoms, nature walks, picnics and pizza making keep younger guests happy.

Teens have their own clubhouse with a tactful semi-supervised choice of activities including diving trips,

The phrase 'as happy as a sandboy' couldn't be more fitting for children visiting the Maldives

beach football, windsurfing, campfire soirees, table tennis, snooker and the normal gamut of Internet and computer games.

The 18,000-square-metre spa has embraced the best money can buy – from crystal steam rooms to airbeds and ice fountains. You have the choice of ESPA, Thai or Ayurvedic methods and the Bastien Gonzalez's foot and leg treatment (not to be confused with a cosmetic pedicure) that left my nails, skin and muscles feeling ten years younger.

A paradise for all

Various off-island excursions are offered. The dhoni trip to find the Secrets of *Tila*, an underwater wonder of fish and corals laying only a metre below the surface, is highly recommended. An hour's snorkelling followed by a feast of salads, tuna, wraps and chocolate brownies. It's a great and safe way for all age groups to experience the endless spectrum offered by this patch of ocean.

Equally fun, the night fishing trip was a great hit. Sailing from the island just as the sun lost its sting, we immediately began tying hooks and weights on to long spools of twine. Within seconds, the dubiously primitive self-made lures had a nibble, and then a tug as the line went taught, followed by thrilled pulling until a very respectable red snapper came aboard, then a grouper and finally a tuna – too big to pull onto the deck.

On and off the island, it's a paradise for all. Reethi does indeed come at a price, which will rule it out for many, but world savvy travellers whose kids have seen it all won't be disappointed. It's fancy, somewhat flamboyant and full of fun.

Other favourite family hotels include: Reethi's sister hotel Kanuhura (less chi-chi but especially good for under-fives) in the beautiful Raa Atoll; the brand new Landaa Giraavaru in northern Baa atoll – where Four Seasons has come up trumps again with a critter camp complete with marine biologist, coconut bowling, croqkick and Blu – the world's most dazzling restaurant (note: rooms on the south of island are preferable for families as the north shore is rocky with a smaller beach). Lastly but by no means least, check out Per Aquum's Maakanaa, an all-villa resort, purpose built for families and their helpers.

opposite **Al fresco dining at the Fanditha Restaurant**   above and right **Night fishing**

IDEAL AGE: 4–17

One&Only Reethi Rah, North Male Atoll, The Maldives
Tel + 960 664 8800
www.oneandonlyresorts.com

130 villas
Beach villas from US$680

KidsOnly Club for children aged four to eleven, open daily
9.00 a.m. – 9.00 p.m. ClubOne for children aged twelve to seventeen,
open every afternoon

Chill and Thrill

A double agenda can be the recipe for holiday disaster – chill-out time for parents and thrill-out time for children are often incompatible. If taking it in turns to entertain the children while your other half catches up on rest sounds like familiar territory then these holidays could provide the remedy. Supervised children's activities and first-rate kids' clubs allow burnt-out mums and dads the opportunity to book some respite time, re-connect and re-energise, intermingled with as much or as little family pleasure as you want.

BEAT THE BLUES

Woolley Grange, England

The perfect retreat is not an easy find. We wanted somewhere both supremely convivial and genuinely accessible that would provide the ideal antidote to our New Year blues. We were after a home-from-home sort of hotel that was not only nirvana for our ten-month baby Bert, but also somewhere for us to recharge and contemplate the year ahead.

Woolley Grange looked like the answer to our prayers. It is one of five hotels in the Luxury Family Hotels group that specialise in pampering parents in a friendly, kids-come-too sort of way. Their other locales include the stylish and contemporary Ickworth House in Suffolk; Moonfleet Manor, a beachside Georgian hideaway in Dorset; the spectacular Fowey Hall in Cornwall; and the majestic Elms hotel in Worcestershire. Despite each hotel's unique character, the accolades pointed to the same ethos, 'to provide a year-round welcome retreat for all members of the family.' Off we went.

Nestled in 120 acres of Wiltshire countryside and eight miles from Bath in the aptly named Woolley Green is the cosy retreat of Woolley Grange. The manor itself was built in 1665 and was the home of landed gentleman, Francis Randolph. During the eighteenth and nineteenth centuries the manor evolved with the increasing prosperity of its resident family, the Baskervilles. Anyone lucky enough to stay these days, will enjoy a beautiful, individually styled house basking in its former glory, with a few contemporary additions.

On arrival, the reception of the hotel felt like the hallway of an eccentric uncle's home, with its wood panelling, leather sofas and velvet upholstery. General manager, Clare Hammond, clearly sees the hotel and staff as an extension of her own home and family, making sure that guests receive a warm welcome the second they step over the threshold. An additional bonus was Peanut, the beautifully patient hotel spaniel, even when a fearless Bert relentlessly pulled his ears.

Anne of Green Gables

As we entered through the enormous oak door, our senses were greeted by a wonderful waft of wood smoke emanating from the drawing room, where we deposited ourselves onto the two huge, lived-in leather sofas by the fire, which became our home for most of the rainy weekend. They were perfectly suited to eating a cream tea and leafing through magazines and newspapers while Bert ran riot in the crèche.

Woolley Grange has twenty-six rooms, all individually decorated, and as you would expect in a building

As we entered through the enormous oak door, our senses were greeted by a wonderful waft of wood smoke

above The drawing room

of this age, there is no uniformity. Though overall they have an Anne of Green Gables feeling to them – wrought iron beds, patchwork quilts, fireplaces and a general sense of old-fashioned comfort. The only exception to this is a new wing, which has been thoughtfully constructed to fit in with the surroundings. There are rooms and apartments of varying sizes decorated with mid-century modern interiors – ideal if you are in two or more parties and want to be near to each other.

The Woolley Bears Den is the hotel's Ofsted-registered children's play area where families can leave babies and children under eight for up to two hours at a time. This was the first time that I had ever left Bert in a crèche, so I was naturally apprehensive about how he'd respond to a strange environment for an hour while I sauntered off for a massage. My worries were put to rest as soon as we entered. Aside from the fact that it was incredibly secure, the room itself was warm, colourful and surprisingly calm. Once in sight of the play area and other children, he couldn't wait to make friends and explore some of the activities

on offer. When I returned to collect him I found him flirting with a fan club of five- to seven-year-old girls all under the supervision of one of the nannies – it was a very special moment as I realised he loved the company of other children and couldn't wait to play with them again the next day.

We returned to the den that evening at five so that Bert could enjoy supper in the company of like-minded souls, relieving me of any 'what's for supper tonight' duty. He wolfed down the pre-ordered Shepherd's Pie, followed by fruit salad and one last play with his newfound entourage. It was at this moment that I realised that once you become a parent the definition of a happy holiday is one where your kids are happy – it really is as simple as that.

For older kids there's a converted barn area called the Hen House which houses a pool table, air hockey machine, table football and video games for the over-eights, so that they don't feel peeved at being left with their younger siblings. This area is unsupervised, but near enough to the main house to be able to keep an eye on things.

Wrought iron beds, patchwork quilts, fireplaces and a general sense of old-fashioned comfort

Important issues

The real icing on the cake was being able to put Bert to bed at night, turn on the baby listening service and enjoy a delicious guilt-free meal in the dining room. If your child does wake up, reception simply let you know so that you can settle your little one before returning to your soiree.

During the weekend we noticed couples relishing the peace and quiet while their children were happily deposited in the Woolley Bears Den or the Hen House. Probably the perfect opportunity to discuss important issues normally relegated to the bottom of the heap in the hectic routine of home life.

Despite it being a wet and relatively chilly weekend in January, families were making use of the bath-like temperature of the outdoor pool, and squeals of delight could be heard as little ones dashed through the cold into the water – in summer months it's undoubtedly the focal point of the hotel and the surrounding terrace is the perfect place for parents to chat and relax while the kids run riot.

The hotel is currently securing plans to build an indoor pool and spa which really will make any winter stay a treat for both kids and parents, and without fail we will be back to enjoy all of its offerings in the heat of summer.

opposite and below right **The Woolley Bears Den**
above right **The Hen House**

IDEAL AGE: 0–12

Woolley Grange Hotel, Woolley Green, Bradford on Avon, Wiltshire BA15 1TX, UK
Tel +44 (0) 1225 864705
www.luxuryfamilyhotels.com

26 rooms
Double rooms from £245, half board

Ofsted registered Woolley Bears Den for children aged nought to eight, open daily from 10.00 a.m. – 4.45 p.m. In addition, the unsupervised Hen House for older children is open at all times

LA PETITE ECOLE

Le Manoir aux Quat' Saisons, England

No one could accuse Raymond Blanc of not being passionate. In fact he's about the most passionate man I've ever met – when it comes to cooking that is, or looking after his sumptuous Manoir aux Quat' Saisons in Oxfordshire.

Just south of Oxford, in a fold of low hills overlooking rich water-meadows and prosperous agricultural farmsteads, the secluded fifteenth-century house was ideally sited between two important Roman roads. Owned by a succession of statesmen and nobility, it was love at first sight for Raymond who bought the house from Lady Cromwell in 1984.

He brought in twenty-five tonnes of compost, waged a war with the rabbits, cleared the jungle of Brussels sprouts and planted the seeds given to him by his father. Raymond's motto, if he had one, would be 'from garden to table' for his kitchen is as much about raw produce as culinary transformation.

Lovingly restored, each of the bedrooms has a different theme inspired by a painting or statue collected by Raymond during his travels around the world. The latest of which is the Lalique room, filled with exquisite pieces of bijou modern opalescent glass. Each room poses a surprise – resulting in a homely feel with devoted individual flair.

After a scrumptious dinner on the first evening, we were allowed a sneak back-of-house preview of what was to come. Walking round the kitchen at ten o'clock, we saw two commis-chefs plucking twitching langoustine from a huge tray and twisting off their heads. Rosie (my eleven-year-old daughter) winced, wondering if she was going to have to repeat the exercise.

She had nothing to worry about. The next morning, donned in chef-whites, aprons and hats, the eight boys and girls (aged between nine and sixteen) began with a tour of the herb garden. 'It's essential you make the connection between eating and growing food', enthused Raymond, wafting a sprig of rosemary under their noses.

If there's a right and a wrong place to awaken gastronomic senses, this English country garden is the equivalent of tasting vintage Krug as your first sip of champagne. Every which way you turn there's countrified perfection: a church tower; circular dovecot; Jacobean chimneys peeping over the immaculate yew hedging; row upon row of neat organic vegetables; sculptures galore and a wildflower garden brimming with cornflowers and baby poppies from Flanders. It all serves as an appetising sight of where your meals are coming from.

Lovingly restored, each of the bedrooms has a different theme inspired by a painting or statue collected by Raymond

above **Raymond leads the way**

'My hotel is not a temple', explains the fast speaking Raymond 'I want little people to trample through and feel at home.' Still cautious, they began to pick and smell their way through the garden, tasting here, looking there, and fingering everything from the giant spiky artichoke to the humble carrot. With all five senses awakened it was back to the kitchen to test the four tastes: an interactive demonstration tasting sweet raspberry jam, acidic lemon, bitter chicory and salty crisps showed them how to use their tongue and not be fooled by deceptive appearances. Chocolate testing (from Dairy Milk to 100 per cent coco solids) was even more fun.

While Raymond oversees the whole day, regularly popping in to check on progress and enjoyment factors, his right-hand man, course director cum child entertainer Steve Bulmer, holds the fort. Like his maestro, Steve's enthusiasm oozes from every pore.

Heaven's kitchen

Lesson one was not to be afraid of the kitchen – translated in this case to an egg catching game and a talk on 'happy chickens'. As they whipped their meringues into shape, both the egg whites and the little group consolidated. Lesson two was how to mix pasta with

above **Sewing basil in the vegetable garden**

your right hand (so you're free to pick your nose with your left, he joked). And so it went on until they'd produced an impressive array of foccaccia, pizza, pea puree, salmon fishcakes, chocolate mousse and Raymond's favourite childhood dessert – Maman Blanc's floating islands.

Forget Hell's Kitchen, this is Heaven's Kitchen. While every second is spent educating and inspiring the junior-chefs, parents are welcome to spectate or relax in the grounds. Most come and go as they wish, as their offspring confidently absorb the simple, rewarding and creative joy of cooking.

'It's my dream, my vision, my life', Raymond enthused to the children – at the end of the day it was their dream too.

The pot of seeded basil the young epicureans took home was really about planting something that would germinate into a growing passion for food. Passion is contagious – and cook they will. Armed with a recipe book and hotline telephone number straight to the kitchen for any emergency questions they left grudgingly. Raymond smiled at his budding prodigies, adding a final note of wisdom, 'the family that eats together, stays together.'

above **Raymond Blanc**   below **Tranquility by the lake**
opposite **Giant artichokes and cooking pasta**

IDEAL AGE: 8–16

Le Manoir aux Quat' Saisons, Church Road, Great Milton, Oxford OX44 7PD, UK
Tel + 44 (0) 1844 278881
www.manoir.com

32 rooms
Double rooms from £380
Children of all ages welcome

La Petite Ecole cooking school for children aged eight to sixteen
One day non-residential course: £200 per child, 8.45 a.m. – 4.30 p.m.

GATEWAY TO THE SUN

Bab Al Shams, Dubai

While man's rhythm is drumming the sound of the beat on the dazzling development on the coast, nature's tempo still defines the serene peace of the desert, where local traditions and culture make a welcome change.

Under an hour from Jumeirah a fresh, palm-fringed oasis has come to life in the middle of the desert. What appears to be a village at first is in fact Bab Al Shams (meaning 'Gateway to the Sun') – a resort that steps back in time to the last century. Based on a traditional Arabic fort its design includes traditional *majlis* sitting areas and marbled courtyards covered in camel footprints, just the right size for children to place their feet and follow the trail. It looks and feels like a life-sized sand castle.

During the day you can choose from a number of child-friendly desert orientated activities or chill out by the swimming pool. One thing all the children beg for is a henna tattoo. Next to the pool, the elaborately painted henna tent is seldom without a customer having their hands or feet emblazoned with swirly patterns.

Children flock together for the daily pony and camel rides that circle the fort, trekking over the dunes. For the more adventurous, and those with strong stomachs,

there's four-wheel-drive dune bashing, but just watching the display as the cars slide and topple was enough for most.

All 115 rooms and suites are contained within the thick fort walls. Interconnecting rooms, ideal for families, use traditional Gulf decor emphasised with natural stone, dark wood and Arabian glasswork. Tiny steps ascend to the alcove-set baths, crafted out of solid stone and lit by flickering candlelight. Ground floor rooms have their own garden, while suites and first floor rooms have balconies or terraces. The low wattage lighting adds to the subdued atmosphere and even children are subliminally hushed.

Silence and stillness of the desert

The excitement of waking up at the coast is replaced by a great sense of calm getting up in the silence and stillness of the desert. Outside the fort's walls peacocks, gazelles and oryx come to quench their thirst in the waterways. Within the ramparts the fort is a labyrinth of passageways and courtyards. At the heart of the resort the courtyard-based Al Forsan restaurant overlooks a palm grove and the *falaj*, a natural water canal. Live cooking stations prepare international cuisine here all through the day. The breakfast

Children flock together for the daily pony and camel rides that circle the fort

above **Desert oasis**

spread is particularly good with dozens of local specialities but don't be surprised if you see camel's milk for your cereal.

Mellow vibrations of classical guitar music reverberate off the sand walls into the nooks and crannies around the Sarab rooftop bar, from where the daily falcon display is best enjoyed. As the sun disappears behind the dunes the *Zaid* whirls a helpless tethered pigeon in giant circles around his body. The falcon dives repeatedly but each time a sudden jerk on the string results in a near miss until the master relents and lets the bird swoop and clench its claws into its prize.

An Arabian night of belly dancing, music and Arabian cuisine prepared on wood-fired stone ovens

is a must. Nestled between the dunes about 300 metres from the resort, the Al Hadheerah restaurant – a mini open-air fort – is reached by following the path lit by flaming torches. Slouched on comfy cushions and Persian rugs, you can enjoy lively Arabic entertainment as the courses come and go. It's a colourful energised evening where children can join in with the dancing and tricks and the starlit setting is magical.

Situated just off one of the courtyards, Sinbad's Kids Club organises fun activities for children. It's mainly used by under fives and a few older children wanting to do some art and escape the midday sun.

For a bit of wilderness pampering the Satori Spa offers a menu of body and facial treatments in its outdoor or indoor rooms. The signature scalp massage

above **The Al Hadheerah restaurant**

uses local oils infused with exotic flowers and fruits to help restore health to the head and scalp, prevent headaches and promote mental clarity.

Interestingly, the humidity is actually lower in the desert than by the sea. Fine desert breezes have always brought the Bedouins to the dunes, so you can allay any misconceptions about unbearable heat.

A symbolic memory of Bab Al Sham's is of three camels standing in a row on the windswept horizon at sunset; their bright covers shimmering under the stars like the biblical image of the three kings.

A world away from the coast's treasure trove of dazzling baubles, Bab Al Shams offers families a magical desert experience true to Dubai's culture and heritage – a camp for Bedouin wannabes crossing the desert in search of comfort and seclusion.

IDEAL AGE: 2–16

Bab al Shams, PO Box 8168, Dubai, UAE
Tel + 971 4 8326699
www.jumeirahbabalshams.com

115 rooms
Junior suites from US$300
Interconnecting rooms available for families with children

Sinbad's Kids Club for children aged two to twelve, open daily 8.00 a.m. – 8.00 p.m.

RUNNING WILD

Vil Uyana, Sri Lanka

For many Sri Lanka's coastline is its main asset but a trip inland through hills and tea plantations to the cultural triangle, made up of Dambulla's painted caves, Polunnaruwa's famous rock temples and statues and the spectacular rock fortress of Sigiriya, is where the island's true heart lies.

Conveniently, the area is also home to Vil Uyana, Jetwing's new and exciting concept of holiday accommodation. The design of the hotel is the brainchild of environmental architect Sunela Jayawardene and comprises twenty-five dwellings set in twenty-three acres of wetlands, lakes and reedbeds and a haven for wildlife. Sunela, who believes that 'in today's world, the greatest luxuries are space and wilderness,' has been inspired by rural and local traditions. 'My inspiration for the land-use and buildings comes from the pre-colonial vernacular architecture of this island. I have seen structures such as these in forgotten villages, deep in the heart of Sri Lanka.' The surrounding paddy fields are farmed by traditional methods of cultivation and harvesting.

We arrived at night and unless you're given precise directions it's difficult to find, situated well off the beaten track with no road signs. But when you arrive you know you're there. Two sleeping stone lions illuminated by torch flames flank the entrance, where you are gracefully welcomed by Vil Uyana staff. Guided across the lake to a silent, pollution-free buggy, you pass various mysterious and romantic looking dwellings, like a magical mystery tour. Once safely delivered to the main building you cross stepping stones into what feels like the last emperor's court surrounded by seemingly floating rooms and majestic pillars, open to the elements of rural Sri Lanka. Across the court is the infinity edged pool, melting into the lake in the midst of snoozing crocodiles. In the distance sits the staggering backdrop of Sigiriya.

Sunela says 'to me, successful architecture is a tranquil shelter that lies seamlessly upon the earth' resulting in innovatively and beautifully designed eco-dwellings. You can choose your environment: marshland, lakeland, forest or paddy fields. The *Jala Mandapa* water dwellings are connected to land by wooden walkways from which you can take a boat around the reserve. The *Vana Avasa* forest dwellings are situated in regenerated groves positioned to create a feeling of privacy and seclusion.

All are extremely generous in size while being in harmony with the environment. Each has its own outside seating area, providing a comfortable and perfect

In today's world, the greatest luxuries are space and wilderness

viewing spot for the local wildlife. Many of the dwellings have their own swimming pools with sun decks facing the paddy fields from which you can watch the crocodiles on the lawn. There's also ample space to add one, two or even three extra beds for kids.

The bathrooms in the forest dwellings are elegantly rustic and are without question exceptional. Huge, open and on different levels, it's as though nature doesn't stop at the entrance but runs right through into the suite. The kids had a very funny time rescuing a chameleon from the pond in our bathroom before it leaped into the bath. A nice little touch is that instead of providing the standard dressing gowns, there are two brightly coloured handloom sarongs in which to wrap yourself after bathing.

Where nature meets mankind

While Vil Uyana is calming, nature lovers will be able to enjoy a huge number of local activities. A deck on the edge of the lake close to the main swimming pool allows kids, armed with information leaflets and competition questions, to indulge in pond dipping. There is even a resident naturalist who is keen to take guests on outings around the property and further afield. For the less lively but no less interested, one of the hotel's floating rooms is a library, well stocked with books on the wildlife and culture of Sri Lanka. A beautiful space, completely open to the elements and surrounded by water, one simply can't resist spending time there.

Of course, the hotel will arrange excursions to all the famous cultural sites. The pick of the bunch has to be Sigiriya. It's quite a climb, but well worth it. Once past the beautiful painted murals of Sri Lankan nymphs, you ascend the summit via a vertiginous iron stairway that clings to the face of the rock. It's best visited at sunrise or sunset but don't forget to take a torch. Vil Uyana also organises hot air balloon rides over the ancient monuments. Or if you prefer something a little more off the beaten track, there are two national parks close by, Mineriya and Kaudule, which offer a variety of safaris. They'll take you to a beautiful na tree forest, the largest in south Asia, or trekking to a pink

left **Vil Uyana style**
opposite **Tea plantation landscape**

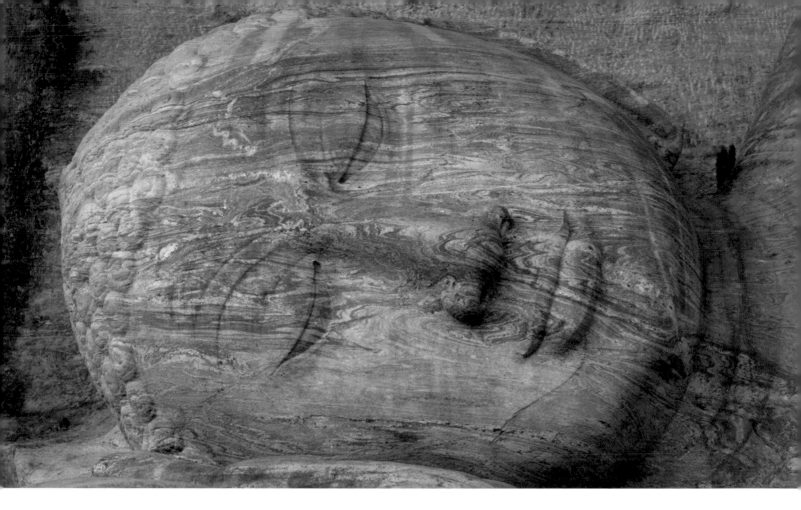

above **The sleeping Buddah**
opposite, (clockwise from top
left) **View from Sigiriya; tea;**
elephants; postcards

quartz rock with a Buddha on top. There are so many excursions that you'll wish you could stay longer.

If this all sounds a little too energetic for you, you could just relax in the peaceful surroundings or lose yourself in the nature of the spa where a selection of massages, facials, wraps and body scrubs are on offer. The spa also has a gym, a yoga pavilion and a resident Ayurvedic doctor who will prescribe a programme or individual traditional treatments for those with a passion for optimum health and rejuvenation.

Preserving and bringing attention to conservation of wildlife is very much the focus of this unusual hotel. It has its own research centre, (with accommodation for passing groups of botanists and zoologists), which aims to educate and raise awareness on the local issues of nature and wildlife.

Vil Uyana is 'a place where nature meets mankind', my ten-year-old son said with profound sagacity. If you are after luxury with an eco flavour and a healthy combination of relaxation, fun and adventure, it's really worth the trip.

IDEAL AGE: 6–16

Vil Uyana
Sigiriya,
Sri Lanka.
Tel: +94 11 5545711
www.viluyana.com

25 rooms
Paddy Field Villa from US$425

Tailor-made nature tours for children – on request

THE EAGLETS HAVE LANDED

Gleneagles, Scotland

It's really saying something about a place when it can host anything, from a momentous G8 summit to an abundance of children looking for nothing but fun and entertainment, with equal poise and dedication. But then again, some might ask, what's the difference between politicians and children?

Gleneagles in Scotland was a pleasant surprise on so many fronts and the number of families present (on a wet off-season weekend) was testimony to the extent and popularity of the all-inclusive activities offered to youngsters. 'We want them to try something they haven't done before,' said development director George Graham, adding 'there are no salutes or shoulder-braids, lunch can take ten minutes or two hours – and nowhere is out of bounds.'

Situated roughly halfway between Edinburgh and Glasgow in a valley surrounded by eye-soothing glens, its name actually means the dell of the church (like *église* in French) and has nothing to do with eagles – which by happy coincidence also inhabit this part of the British Isles. As constructions go (with 232 bedrooms) it's a bit of a monster from certain angles; typical of that 1920s era when men like Donald Matheson (general manager of Caledonian Railway Company) built grand railway hotels around the world.

However, after several multi-million pound refurbishments Gleneagles has never looked better; and for young visitors fun comes with a capital F. Run more like an adventure camp than a kids' club, its ingenuity and enthusiasm stems from the staff, who are as eager to make fun as the children are to expend their energy.

On the ground floor part of the Club (the leisure and health wing of the hotel) has been transformed into a dedicated zone for tots-to-teens. Adolescents, so often overlooked in holiday hotels, have their own area with everything from pool table to plasma and PS3s in a chill-out area with giant beanbags, SingStar and a self-service fruit bar. For the over sixteens, the Club's other facilities include fully equipped gym, sauna, steam-room, stylish spa and three swimming pools, including a lap, leisure and outdoor 'hot' pool with Jacuzzi jets.

Younger children can enjoy painting and modelling activities in the creative area, complete with sandpit, dressing up, doll's house and cooking station. The impressive ever-changing curriculum means that weeks are themed into seasonal interests where children can plant sunflowers, make autumnal mobiles and seeded bird-cakes, have a pow-wow round their

Run more like an adventure camp than a kids' club, its ingenuity and enthusiasm stems from the staff

above **Junior off-road driving**
opposite **Gleneaglets at play**

own totem poles, be boat builders, master mariners or Scottish inventors. They can compete in 'Ready Steady Cook', have a space hopper race through the maze, or just fool around with some horseplay on hand-modelled hobbyhorses.

The great outdoors

Outdoor sports hold the real appeal for Gleneagles – and having the freedom and safety to go where you please are key ingredients on the 850-acre estate, a huge playground by anyone's standard, enjoying unparalleled diversity.

Gleneagles golf is an unashamed pleasure and with names like James Braid and Jack Nicklaus running through its blood it's no surprise that the famous PGA Centenary Course has been selected as the venue for the 2014 Ryder Cup. Junior golf lessons are available at the Academy, where budding Tiger Woods receive their own clubs (cut to suit height and swing), and are videoed and photographed during action. The pitch and putt in front of the hotel was full of young golfers putting their new found learning into practice.

The junior off-road driving was a huge thrill. My daughter tested her driving skills in the mini Land Rover, bumping over log-piles, through waterlogged trenches narrowly missing flags and obstacles, on the purpose built track designed to mimic the grown up course.

Handling and flying a bird of prey came next at the resident British School of Falconry. After an introduction to the noisy Peregrine falcons Bubble and Squeak (which can hit their prey at a staggering 240mph), and Fatty the majestic golden eagle (a comparatively slow, moody and clumsy bird, afraid of pushchairs), we ventured out with the endearing Jerry, a ten-month-old Harris hawk. 'How much can he eat?' asked my daughter. 'About the same as four fish fingers a day', Alan the falconer replied in helpful child-speak. We watched the measuring and weighing of the birds on old-fashioned scales and marked their flying target on the chart. We learnt that it's an enjoyable sport based on precision and intimacy as Jerry followed us around the grounds returning to our leather gloved hands when beckoned.

Fly fishing,
archery and rifle
shooting for
the over eights
and clays for
over tens are
very popular

Sleeping well

The impressive Activities School encompasses shooting, fishing and equestrian pursuits. Fly fishing, archery and rifle shooting for the over eights and clays for over tens are very popular for parents and children alike as are the riding lessons. In the indoor arena our teacher Diana kept us busy with exercises including a nice rising trot, circus style (with arms out at three and nine o'clock), tiptoeing over jump poles and cantering large circles on Jamie, a fluffy Shetland, and Pugsy, a gentle sixteen-hand giant, so safe he's had six-year-olds on his back.

With all this physical activity it is essential to recharge your batteries at regular intervals. On the culinary front, the various restaurants feature the best of local Scottish fare. The Young Guns and Just for

Kids menus offer a good variety of healthy, well-priced options but you're just as likely to see children tucking into a junior serving of oak smoked salmon or Beef Wellington. High chairs intermingle effortlessly with silver cloches and Michelin stars, and anything is possible whether on or off the menu.

While there's enough to keep you busy on the estate for a least a week, local cultural attractions including the Wallace monument (think *Braveheart*), Stirling Castle (James VI), the ruined remains of Linlithgow Palace (birthplace of Mary Queen of Scots) and Edinburgh are all under an hour's drive away.

It's clear that children of all ages just love the place and if you're an active sort of parent, a holiday here could turn into a second childhood. One thing's for sure, you'll certainly all sleep well.

Falconry and golf lessons

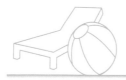

IDEAL AGE: 2 –16

The Gleneagles Hotel, Auchterarder, Perthshire,
Scotland PH3 1NF
Tel + 44 (0) 1764 662231
www.gleneagles.com

232 rooms
Double rooms from £285

The Gleneaglets Kids' Club playroom for children aged
two to ten, open daily 9.30 a.m. – 5.30 p.m. In addition
there's a huge variety of outdoor activities for children
of all ages

HOME SWEET HOME

Ballymaloe House, Ireland

The approach to the wisteria-clad Georgian manor said it all. We had to stop down the long drive, bursting with banks of blossoming rhododendron, to allow dishevelled looking ewes, attending their pristine fluffy white lambs, to pass. As we turned the corner the house came into view; it appeared deliciously ramshackle in a country house 'lived-in' sort of way. 'Hmmm, I wonder how child friendly it is,' I thought. Then I spotted a couple of boys no older than six playing a boisterous game of croquet on a lawn littered with daisies in front of the rather grand façade, and I knew we'd come to the right place.

Before we had even stepped over the hearth the children had spied the swimming pool, tennis court, bicycles, sandpit, swings, slide, boys up the trees, golf course, peacocks and coops of turkeys and chickens. The Irish welcome was as genteel and unstuffy as ever and put us instantly at ease.

I first heard about Ballymaloe from Nigel Chapman, who told me that south-east Ireland was where he'd found the model on which he designed his successful group Luxury Family Hotels – now a tried and tested formula for chilled-out thrills for the whole family. Chilled out for guests, normally means feverish activity behind-the-scenes for staff, and the Allen's

story is no exception. If necessity is the mother of invention, Ballymaloe's success lies in its history.

The sprightly octogenarian Myrtle Allen tells how she grew up across the bay and used to whistle to the harbour master for a boat to take her to 'my love' in Shanagarry. Love blossomed and once married, her husband Ivan bought the big house 'that nobody wanted' in 1948 and began to farm and raise a family.

With six hungry children to feed, rapid inflation and new licensing laws, hard times in the 1960s left Myrtle and Ivan Allen no alternative but to open their house and their dining room to paying guests. They served what they ate – delicious home-cooked food sourced from their farm and garden. Before long, it grew from a thriving bed and breakfast into today's thirty-four-bedroom hotel.

As it flourished, Myrtle began sharing homespun recipes through her writing and teaching and one day a student completed her course and fell in love with one of the Allen boys. Four decades later, Darina is as big a celebrity as Myrtle and Ballymaloe is a hotbed of culinary excellence, a powerhouse that occupies the whole extended family. Myrtle's son Rory and daughter-in-law Hazel run the hotel; Wendy runs the shop; Fawn, the reception; Yasmin makes pickles, and

The children spied the swimming pool, tennis court, bicycles, sandpit, swings, slide and boys up the trees

various grandchildren chip in wherever needed. A family affair through and through, Rory even entertains guests after dinner playing Irish ditties on his mandolin.

Local, seasonal produce

Internationally renowned for its food, or as the chatelaine of the house might say, 'good ingredients that don't need messing with,' the menu never disappoints. Organic herbs and vegetables from the kitchen garden; cheese and meat from local dairy herds; and fish from the boats at Ballycotton harbour – it champions local, seasonal sources; a dying trend in a society that expects asparagus in December. A new dinner menu is written every afternoon based on what has been brought into the kitchen from the garden, butcher and pier that day. Children can opt for high tea in the conservatory, with unfussy favourites like free-range chicken and chips followed by meringue and ice cream. While breakfast, fit for an emperor, consists of freshly baked breads, including local soda loaf; sweet berries, apricots and prunes; apple muesli; porridge; Irish kippers; and fresh gooseberry preserve.

An overriding sense of calm oozes from every nook and cranny of the house at Ballymaloe. During the day, the perfectly proportioned living rooms are silent save for distant birdsong or an occasional peacock cry. While bedrooms are charmingly homey and restful, don't expect any television – take a good book and savour the peace. It's shabby chic at its best.

There are plenty of pursuits for sunny or rainy (as is often the case) days both on and around the estate. Whatever the weather, you'd do well to spend an afternoon at Darina's famed cookery school and pick up some of her culinary genius. It's hard to capture the sheer joy of dreamily wandering about Darina's grounds. Each garden room presenting something new and exciting: the fruitery, herbery, vegetable potager, shell palace, hen house, lake, dragonery, herbaceous avenue and Celtic maze bestowing ecstatic escapism for children darting excitedly from one to the other.

below left **Egg hunt**
oppposite **Herb garden**

Try kite flying opposite Ireland's handsomest lighthouse or a blustery walk collecting winkles and lugworms along the five miles of sandy beach, or a visit to Stephen Pearce's local pottery. The Pearces and Allens can't remember who started cooking or pottery first but share childhood memories of 'Tommy Sliney's donkey and cart selling fish and running barefoot along un-tarred roads lined with an abundance of sweet-smelling flowers, blackberries, crab apples, damsons and field mushrooms.'

Fresh air, freedom and fun

In the natural harbour of Cobh (pronounced Cove) you can retrace the routes of trade ships, passenger liners and men 'o' war since the early seventeenth century. Over four million people have emigrated from this inconspicuous waterfront over the years in search of better futures, although it's probably best remembered as the last port of call for the ill-fated maiden voyage of RMS *Titanic*. Further-afield, you can visit an arboretum, wildlife park, Barry's Court Castle, or go whale watching in Kinsale, and Cork is under an hour away.

Ballymaloe's magic lies in the surrounding fields, rocky inlets, cliff walks and lonely headlands, loved most by those who live there and continue to take happiness in sharing it with all generations. It epitomises a yesteryear kind of escapism for children, who have the space and freedom to roam as they wish, soon making friends and playing games with other guests or Allen grandchildren. Fresh air, freedom and fun are the key ingredients.

above **Shell collecting on Shanagarry beach**

Ballymaloe's magic lies in the surrounding fields, rocky inlets, cliff walks and lonely headlands

IDEAL AGE: 4–16

Ballymaloe House, Shanagarry, Co Cork, Ireland
Tel +353 (0) 21 465 2531
Fax +353 (0) 21 465 2021
www.ballymaloe.ie

34 rooms
Double rooms from €220, half board

No kids' club but children are welcome to join in with all the activities on offer

ON THE WILD SIDE

Spain

Spain has long been Europe's most popular holiday destination for the sun and sangria generation. And for good reason, you cannot beat the beaches, the sunbathing, swimming in warm, calm, clear waters, diving down to the colourful seabed, or exploring the coastline by boat. All in a country where the family has deep-rooted respect reflected in the daily way of life, and the fact that tourists of all ages receive a warm welcome.

Spain has a lot more than this to offer. Behind the coast lies a huge interior full of lakes, mountains, rivers, valleys and plateaus, which together with the country's warm climate makes its natural history a joy for families to explore. In recent years the public's burgeoning interest in nature and conservation has seen Spain redevelop some of its National Parks, opening some of the finest nature reserves and theme parks in the world.

Add to the mix the chain of superb state-funded Paradores de Turismo hotels spanning the country and you can start to see the bones of a wonderful holiday. The Paradores, often restored historic buildings and castles, staffed by knowledgeable locals serving high-quality regional cuisine, provide more than a simple resting place.

Myriad locations across the interior offer popular outdoor activities such as hiking, skiing, sailing, fishing, biking and riding. But it is only by visiting one of the hidden jewels, such as Doñana in Andalucia in the south, Cabárceno in Cantabria in the north, or the region now known as Europe's Jurassic Park in nearby La Rioja that you can get a true taste of Spain's wild side.

Natural jewel

In ancient times the mouth of the Guadalquivir, Andalucia's mightiest river, was a wide lagoon dotted with islands, one of which is said to have been the capital of the mythical kingdom of Tarshish. Gradually the area silted up, giving way to a landscape of marshes, shifting sand dunes and pine forests. In the sixteenth century it was the hunting ground of kings, lorded over by the powerful Duke of Medina Sidonia, and became known – in honour of the Duke's wife – as Doña Ana. Today, protected as the Doñana National Park, it is one of Europe's most valuable natural jewels. Located an hour south of Seville, its mosaic of landscapes and unique biodiversity offer a lush wetland home to over 300 species of birds that use it as a mating ground and a stopping place on long migratory routes. The park is

Behind the coast lies a huge interior full of lakes, mountains, rivers, valleys and plateaus

also a refuge for a number of animals like red deer, bucks and wild boar, the endangered Imperial Eagle and Iberian Lynx.

There are many ways to tour the park, which is entered via one of the free visitor centres. One is to use the meandering wooden walkways where children can break for pit stops that take in fabulous views and read the educational panels. Or you could choose to follow the routes by bike, on horseback, in an all-terrain bus or even by boat.

The Parador de Mazagón, on the coast near Huelva, provides the perfect base for a visit to Doñana. Set in large gardens and surrounded by pine trees, many of the rooms have terraces that look directly onto the calm waters of this coast. The restaurant specialises in local fish dishes using shrimps, prawns and cockles. From the mountains inland come cured hams from Jabugo and Iberian pâtés or try the chef's main speciality, tasty local pork.

If you like your children's activities to be organized for you, there are two places, both in northern Spain, that really have to be recommended. The impressive Cabárceno Nature Park in the Cantabrian Mountains about half an hour from Santander extends over 750 hectares making it the largest nature park in Europe. It has all the attractions to match. Exotic animals such as Bengal tigers roam in vast kilometre-long enclosures alongside desert antelopes and African elephants. It's a zoo as you've never seen or dreamt of. 'All zoos should be like this,' my six-year-old piped as she walked among the ostriches, watched the majestic lions, stealthy jaguars and impressive rhinos. There are more than 118 species living in the park, along with their juveniles, given that this is one of the few enclosed places on earth where animals reproduce naturally. The park's

network of asphalted roads make for an easy drive-through, but there are more experiential alternatives including walking trails and bicycle routes.

Europe's Jurassic Park

In the region of La Rioja, near Logroño, now known as Europe's Jurassic Park the evidence of dinosaur activity is strong. It is home to a huge number of dinosaur-based attractions including several palaeontology centres, which mark the start of family-friendly adventure trails. Located in open countryside these trails are well signposted, have easy vehicle or pedestrian access, and information panels that help you absorb everything en route. There are also specialist guide services posted along the forty sites, from Era del Peladillo in Igea, Europe's most popular dinosaur site, to Conargo's superb prehistoric footprints.

Close by, in Soria, you can learn about Jurassic habits at the Villar del Río Palaeontological Centre. Travelling a little further north, in Asturias, the coastal towns of Villaviciosa, Colunga and Ribadesella form a famous dinosaur route culminating in the Dinópolis theme park at Teruel.

There are a number of Paradores in the area but the Santillana Gil Blas in Santillana del Mar, now a national monument and one of the most beautiful historical villages in Spain, has good access to both Cabárenco and the dinosaur routes.

Spain has many advantages for the travelling family: it has easy access, warm temperatures are guaranteed, children are welcome everywhere and the food is attractive to adults and little ones alike. Look beyond the beaches, and you will be rewarded with a holiday that fills you and your children's dreams with rare natural wonders that are Spain's best kept secret.

previous page **The Parador at Santillana del Mar, and the beauty of Doñana**
right **The Dinópolis museum at Teruel in Asturias**
opposite (clockwise from top left) **Sand-dunes and birds at Doñana, the strange limestone landscape at Cabárceno, prehistoric foo-prints, wetland biodiversity at Doñana, elephants roaming in the Cantabrian mountains**

IDEAL AGE: 4–16

There are Parador hotels throughout the country
Rates vary
Tel: +34 902 54 79 79
www.parador.es
www.spain.info

JOIN THE CLUB

All inclusive resorts in Italy and Greece

The truth about successful family holidays is simple. If the children are happy and having a good time, then the parents enjoy themselves too, sometimes at the expense of culture, privacy and tranquillity. One formula that has hit the spot for families in recent years has been the one-stop-shop, all-inclusive, village-style holiday. These holidays are aimed at families in search of a choice of accommodation, a choice of restaurants and bars and, most importantly of all, a wide range of organised activities for children of all ages and on-tap nursery and babysitting facilities.

Forte Village in Sardinia is often mentioned as the ultimate family-style holiday resort, an easy solution that ticks all those boxes in one fell swoop. The sun always shines, the food is good, the variety of accommodation is excellent and the activities on offer are breathtaking, but they come at a price. There's one thing everyone should know before booking a holiday at Forte Village – it requires deep pockets.

Making friends and running free

When we holidayed there a few years' ago, our children then aged nine, six and four had the time of their lives, and remember it still with such fondness that there's a part of me that believes there has been no holiday before or since quite like it. By day they rode bikes, played football, slid down giant slides, went trampolining, go-karting, banana-boating and swimming; by night they ate pizza and candyfloss and watched starlit performances of mini West End Shows at the central piazza. They made friends and ran free.

Funnily enough their feeling of freedom paralleled the adults feeling of mild claustrophobia. Forte Village is a self-contained microcosm of non-stop fun and happiness and there is no reason to step beyond its boundaries while you are there. In total it's a fifty-four-acre site, within which at peak times exist a maximum of about 1,500 guests with staff numbers to match. Peace and quiet doesn't come readily, (except in the Thalassotherapy Spa which, incidentally, is excellent) and you can never escape other people.

There's also an interesting concept of hierarchy. Of the Village's seven hotels, three of them (the Castello, Le Dune and Villa del Parco) are five star, and four (Il Villagio, Le Palme, La Pineta and Il Borgo) are four star. The restaurants – all twenty-one of them, and that doesn't include the bars – work on a similar basis, whereby if you're a five-star guest you can eat in any of them, but if you're a four-star guest you have

Forte Village is a self-contained microcosm of non-stop fun and happiness

previous page **Kassandra beach, Porto Sani**   above **Porto Sani pool and marina**   opposite **Mini Club fun and seaside tranquility**

The Sani Asterias Suites themselves are well designed in that muted palette so popular of late

to pay a supplement to eat in the posher ones. Oddly enough, no one seems to mind.

A couple of years ago, in search of a similar experience to Forte Village, but without the cost, we visited Porto Sani on the Halkidiki peninsula in Greece. At the time Porto Sani had just launched its Sani Asterias Suites, a five-star boutique hotel, one of four hotels within the resort. In this instance, two (the Sani Beach Club and the Sani Beach Hotel) describe themselves as four-star (an optimistic rating, I'd say) while the Porto Sani Village is five-star but on a larger scale and, crucially, without direct beach access.

The Sani Asterias Suites themselves are well designed in that muted palette so popular of late. The best rooms have private gardens and open directly onto the beach, while others overlook the pool (for exclusive use of SAS guests) and the marina. And it's

the marina that makes this place really interesting not simply because of the boats but more because of the shops and restaurants that line its waterfront. Porto Sani welcomes in the outside world in a way that Forte Village doesn't. At night the marina buzzes with as many locals as hotel guests who come to eat, drink, shop or yacht spot. Although you can eat at the SAS's own very good restaurant, we chose most nights to amble off round the marina where the children could run freely and safely.

While Sani's upmarket bits are better than Forte's, its downmarket bits are worse. As comfortable as you feel cocooned at the Suites there is no escaping the big, white monolith of the Beach Hotel just a few hundred metres away. They could also do with a few more tennis courts and activities, particularly for older children. But as ever it's a rolling programme and each year brings new additions and upgrades.

In terms of upgrades the resort to watch is Chia Laguna, also in Sardinia and not more than a few miles away from Forte Village. This could be the hotel that knocks Forte off its pedestal, but it's still a year or two from achieving this.

Right now Chia Laguna consists of one resort with two levels of accommodation – the Village and the deluxe Hotel. The former are cottage-style rooms strung out throughout the grounds and linked by cobbled roads, while the latter comprises one building containing some recently (and very tastefully) refurbished rooms. There are five restaurants (including a handy takeway pizzeria), which operate on a similar hierarchical system to those at Forte (Village people, for example, can't join in the buffet at the Hotel) and a similar piazza with smart boutiques and a stage for nightly shows. Football, biking, and kids' clubs are all on offer.

The beach is both the pleasure and the pain of Chia Laguna. First and foremost it is exquisite – one of the best beaches I've seen in the Mediterranean – but sadly the hotel is divided from it by a fairly major road and about half a mile of track. To shuttle guests to and from the beach there's a carriage-pulling vehicle disguised as a train, which trundles back and forth (much to young children's utter delight). The beach, of course, is busy with rows of sunbeds and umbrellas (hotel guests, by the way, have priority over the front two rows) but the sea is lovely. There's also a great beach restaurant, which means no to-ing and fro-ing back to the hotel in the middle of the day.

The plans for Chia Laguna's makeover are extensive, ranging from a new pool for hotel guests only, a new restaurant, new tennis courts and a bigger, better spa. Slightly longer term will be the equestrian centre, a pedestrian walkway over the road and the construction of a super deluxe, suite-only hotel on a hillside right by the sea. It will definitely be worth waiting for.

left **Life in Forte Village**
opposite **The Mediterranean at Chia Laguna**

opposite **Village life offers guaranteed fun for children**   above **Sani Asterias pool and suites behind**

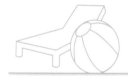

Forte Village Resort, Santa Margherita di Pula, Cagliari, Sardinia, Italy
Tel + 39 (0) 709 2171
www.fortevillageresort.com

7 hotels
Rates vary

Crèche for children aged nought to two years, open daily, Mini Club for children aged two to eleven, open daily 9.00 a.m. – 1.00 p.m and 2.00 p.m. – 6.00 p.m. and a Junior Club for twelve to seventeen year olds offers a daily sports programme (May to September)

Sani Resort, 630 77 Kassandra, Halkidiki, Greece
Tel + 30 23740 99400
www.saniresort.gr

50 Asterias Suites
Rates vary

Melissa Mini Club for children aged four to twelve, open daily, offers morning and afternoon activity programmes. There is an organised teenage club for children aged thirteen to sixteen during the high season

Chia Laguna, Localita Chia Domus de Maria Cagliari, Sardinia 09010
Tel + 39 (0) 709 239 3420
www.chialagunaresort.it

372 rooms
Rates vary

The Children's Club for children aged three to twelve, open daily 9.00 a.m. – 1.00 p.m and 3.30 p.m. – 6.00 p.m. (June to September)

HELL IS THE NEW HEAVEN

Hell Bay Hotel, Scilly Isles

'Two thousand alcoholics clinging to a rock', was how the jolly harbour master in Tresco described the Scilly Isles' inhabitants – and while we didn't see a single drunk, the Scillonions are a cheery group and certainly know how to enjoy the good life.

Situated at the south-westerly tip of the British Isles, twenty-eight miles from the Cornish mainland, Scilly makes for an unexpected paradise. Lashed by Atlantic breakers and warmed by the Gulf Stream you'd be forgiven for thinking you were in the Caribbean.

Of the 120 islands, only five (St Mary's, Tresco, Bryher, St Martin and St Agnes) are inhabited – the rest remain an untouched landscape and a sanctuary for wildlife. To holiday here is like returning to a charming episode of adventure from the last century. Arrival, more often than not, is on one of the eighteen-seater, twin otter, propeller planes that leave from the basic-but-efficient regional airports such as Bristol, Exeter or St Mawes. When the passengers have chosen their seats, the pilots clamber aboard, shut the door and excuse themselves as they squeeze past to reach the open-view cockpit. Then it's chocks away and up into the headwinds.

Journeying in this manner is a good indicator of what a visit to Scilly is all about; a sort of friendly travellers' bond is formed – a rare occurrence in a world often too busy to care. Everyone seems automatically to adopt a kind of old-fashioned concern and politeness that so typifies the hospitality of the islands.

From the one-storey terminal on St Mary's, a driver, who waves to every passer-by, takes you down to the port to catch the boat across the channel to Bryher. With such a small population, everyone seems to know everyone. What's more, there's no crime, no danger and generally speaking, no rush. Houses are left open, bicycles are never padlocked and children of all ages can roam around un-chaperoned.

For children, Scilly offers a twenty-first century *Swallows and Amazons* type existence, packed with adventure and imaginative discovery. For adults, a day on Scilly is worth at least two days anywhere else. Everything just feels so relaxed.

The islands are run as a self-governing unitary authority reporting directly to a political Dias with a chief executive – giving it an independent air that feels like a cross between a private members club and the film *Passport to Pimlico*. One of the key beauties is that it has a finite number of beds – so when it's full, it's full.

The wind-worn ruggedness of Bryer is so different from the closeted protection of Tresco; it comes as

To holiday here is like returning to a charming episode of adventure from the last century

above **Harbour master**
opposite **Tresco's Abbey Gardens**

The relaxed informality and the personal care of the staff add to the overall feeling of wellbeing at Hell Bay

quite a surprise. While Tresco remains by far the best known of all the islands (mainly because of its fabulous Abbey Gardens), Bryher acts as a windbreak for Tresco, protecting her from the ferocious prevailing currents that sweep across the Atlantic.

New kid on the block

If the Island Hotel on Tresco is the old lady of Scilly, the new kid on the block is Bryher's Hell Bay Hotel – of the one-island, one-hotel variety. Robert Dorrien-Smith inherited the bankrupt, worn-out, mile-square island at the age of twenty-three with a vision of, 'turning it into a diamond'. He has succeeded. Today's fine balance between encouraging low-impact tourism and maintaining traditional daily life means the sixty-strong community is thriving. Local children attend the primary school on Tresco to the age of thirteen and then go on to secondary school on St Mary's (the UK's only state funded boarding school) from Monday to Friday. Most then choose to return to carve a life on the islands.

I couldn't track down an authoritative source on why it's called Hell Bay but the number of ships that have sunk on the dramatic granite crags along the shoreline has captured the minds of many an author and at night the rock is lit up by a roaming searchlight from the lighthouse across the bay.

The relaxed informality and the personal care of the staff add to the overall feeling of wellbeing at Hell Bay. Each of the hotel's twenty-five suites, named after an island gig, has its own sea-facing balcony or terrace and is comfortably decorated with local paintings, sculptures and Lloyd Loom furniture in a nautical-cum-Ralph Lauren style. Bleached clapboard exteriors merely add to Bryher's New England ambiance. During the summer months, the heated outdoor pool is a popular spot, although nothing beats the thrill of the beach.

Food, served by antipodeans (shipped in to help during the busiest months), is healthy, hearty and based on top quality ingredients that don't need tarting up. So long as the weather permits, the *Lioness Lady* docks into St Mary's three times a week to deliver provisions for all the islanders and their guests. 'We've never let anyone starve,' jokes manager Euan Rodger. Most diners choose fish – the fresh crab, lobster and shellfish are handpicked from the daily catch and taste exquisite.

There's plenty to discover whether you're a walker, birder, sailor, artist, gardener or sunbed seeker. Each morning children jump out of bed, hurriedly dress and set off on an adventure. With practically no roads, people get around by bicycle or tractor but exploring by boat is the mainstay of family holidays.

Where did the Whales Go?

The shiny white sands of St Martins resemble an equatorial paradise, while the whole area is home to a fascinating array of wildlife including, large numbers of puffins, hoopoes and bald sea eagles.

For a real adventure, climb onto the mighty *Cyclone*, a 24-foot rib complete with 500-horsepower engine.

With the agility of a ballet dancer the skipper can make the rib pirouette around the rocks and lighthouses a mere arm-length from gannets, cormorants, seals and if you're very lucky, dolphins. It gives a better understanding of the islands, their vulnerability to the elements and their sheer unspoilt beauty.

Scilly is great for all ages but particularly fun for families who have finished the chapter of chasing after runaway toddlers. Friendly little gangs of plucky children, un-awed by the opportunity to create their own adventure, spring up all over the islands. And before you can say 'where did the whales go?' they have assumed character names with a mission to explore.

Hell in this case is certainly heaven.

IDEAL AGE: 4-16

Hell Bay Hotel, Bryher, Isles of Scilly, TR23 0PR, UK
Tel + 44 (0) 1720 422947
www.hellbay.co.uk

25 suites
Double rooms from £130 per person per day half board
Interconnecting rooms available

No kids' club but the RYA recognised sailing school
caters for all levels and ages of sailor

TIP
· *Your kids will love it if you take a copy of* Why the Wales Came *by Michael Morpurgo*

YAHOOING ON THE AEGEAN

Sunsail's Club Phokaia, Turkey

You wake up, fling open the French windows, inhale the fresh morning air from the balcony and take in the view: swimming pool, check; lush gardens, check; coruscating azure sea, check; bloke wandering around watering the flowerbeds, check. In a couple of minutes, you reach the heart of your hotel complex, and sit on the terrace breakfasting on coffee, fresh fruit, an omelette, made al fresco in front of your eyes.

Yep, it's all there: everything we need for a holiday that will be about as nerve-racking as stroking a kitten on Valium. An hour later, though, it is apparent that Sunsail's Club Phokaia near Foca in western Turkey will be a bit more of an adventure. My mucker Matthew and I are hanging out of a sailing dinghy bouncing across an aggressive little chop as we get out into the bay.

Twenty knots of wind sends spray flying over the boat as we crash over another wave. Matthew, hanging on the trapeze – a wire from the mast on which he suspends himself to get his weight right out of the boat – makes a suggestion, 'Shall we get the kite up?' (The kite being a reaching sail that will instantly double the square feet we have in front of the wind.) The boat skitters and jumps in a gust. 'Er, OK, sure, let's give it a go.'

Seconds later, after much frantic pulling, hands bleeding from a burst blister created on an earlier excursion, our little Laser Vago is doing all it can to take off with twenty-six stones of bloke straining and tensing to keep the thing upright. With a lung-busting 'Yaaaahoo', the boat goes into overdrive; we've tamed the beast, the sea is hissing and fizzing beneath us, and two men, a concoction of stainless steel and fibreglass, the wind and the sea are in harmony.

Well, for a few minutes, anyway. A goliath of a gust overpowers us, the boat crashes arse-over-tip into the sea, and the dads bob up and down in the water disentangling themselves from the melee of ropes. Within a minute, a chirpy chap with salt-encrusted sunglasses turns up in a safety boat to check all is well. It is. And off we go to do it all over again.

This is adventure all right, but it is adventure-lite. Here I can satisfy a lifelong lust for sailing that included running a sailing centre in Greece and pass on that passion to my children without forcing them to endure chilly exhortations to heave on sodden ropes in the murk of the Thames. Furthermore, in a couple of hours, Matthew and I will be in the bar.

Showered, refreshed (although with windswept skin the colour of pimento), we will be reunited with our

With a lung-busting 'Yaaaahoo', the boat goes into overdrive

Beginners and the more experienced sailors

My elder
daughter, eyes
sparkling, and
I were skitting
across the waves

wives and children who as members of the kids' clubs, Sea Urchins, Gybers, etc, depending on their ages, will have had their own adventures in the briny and oh, the tales that we'll tell of our exploits at sea. How steadfastly we hiked hard and trimmed the sails to prevent a hurricane-force gust sweeping us over; how only well-timed teamwork prevented us from skewering the incompetents sailing by on one of the yachts; how in an act of extreme bravery we picked ourselves up from another capsize and headed out to sea again.

Sailing any way you want

Club Phokaia offers adventure in spades. Team up with another family, go yacht cruising. Take your children out of the club and go off sailing together; race against other sailors; teach your own children to sail; or, for some families, for whom Club Phokaia is simply a fairly luxurious hotel in a beautiful setting, get someone else to teach them for you.

Or do all of it. Even if you're a beginner or a relatively inexperienced sailor, you can take advantage of an operation so well drilled you almost expect to see little sergeant-majors popping out from behind the palms barking orders to the sailing instructors.

Within seconds, a bright orange Funboat was rigged and on the water, and in the same brisk wind, on the same dark Aegean water, my elder daughter, eyes sparkling, and I were skitting across the waves. Golly it

was fun helping her guide this splendid little craft out to sea, valiantly holding its own in surprisingly strong breezes while racing thoroughbreds crashed and burned around us.

The whole family, too, took off on one of the ten big, gutsy Hobie catamarans, whooping with delight as we got a hull airborne and sped out to sea waving at instructors joyriding beginners on the same craft.

Club Phokaia has about a million dinghies, nine yachts for day sailing and racks full of windsurfers at your disposal. It is a truly Noughties institution, where everyone says 'hi guys' to everyone. You can work out in the gym, get pampered in the spa, or take one of the mountain bikes out alone or in a group into the Turkish hinterland. It's a regime that will satisfy the dilettante, the novice, the expert.

Do you mind if we join you?

If, however, you're not so sociable, you might find the atmosphere a bit too much. Socialising is an integral part of a Sunsail Club holiday, but rather than sharing your tales of adventure with a few friends in a bivouac at the side of Ben Nevis, you are expected, even obliged, to meet up with complete strangers on the sun terrace of this private holiday complex.

Sunsail has a unique meals system, but effectively it's halfboard, and some. If you don't want to spend money on cabs and dinner going into Foca two miles or so away, and you'd be mad not to enjoy this unutterably charming, really quite untouristy Turkish town at some point, then you will sit on tables of a minimum of eight. A quiet drink at the bar is impossible: the average time for a 'Do you mind if we join you?' is about three seconds. Whether you do or not, it's not really up to you, and your new drinking partners will set the tone for the evening.

And we had the added problem that while Phoebe, seven, desired nothing more than to join the Sea Urchins for back-to-back adventures, including sailing, mask making, swimming and speedboat rides, Amelia, five, found such enforced fun anathema. She wanted to be with her family. Family, though, was minus big sister, which meant one parent pootling around the swimming pool or beach with a child who was, simply, scared of sailing, which in turn meant parents couldn't go out in a boat together, cue yahooing with Matthew instead. The clubbiness of a Sunsail holiday, in other words, applies to children, too.

All round fun

But these superbly run centres are called Sunsail Clubs, and that should be taken literally. It would be churlish to resent the fact that here is somewhere to make friends (which tends to be with families in the holiday season and couples and singles outside it). Indeed, many families who had met on previous holidays had rebooked together, and enjoyed a boozy, al fresco conviviality, especially with the children safely in video club (until ten o'clock, when babysitting is offered).

The following morning's start to the day, then, is tempered slightly by the prospect of a hangover but nothing that a good dunking can't cure.

You can work out in the gym, get pampered in the spa, or take one of the mountain bikes out

IDEAL AGE: 0–17

Sunsail Clubs, The Port House, Port Solent, Portsmouth, Hampshire PO6 4PH, UK
Tel + 44 (0) 870 427 0077
www.sunsail.co.uk

From £579 per adult and £459 per child for seven days, includes return flights, accommodation, halfboard and use of sailing and shore-based equipment

Magical Mystery

Sometimes only an adventure will fit the
bill and if the saying 'a change is as good as
a rest' suits your mood then these out-of-
the-ordinary family forays will certainly
whet your appetite. They are all on-the-go
type holidays that bring the family together
with joint activities and thrills. Kids' clubs,
lie-ins and lazy afternoons are not on the
menu. Check your energy levels, then it's
on your markies, get your car keys, GO.
Go and see more than you ever knew
existed, go and do more than you ever
thought you could fit in a lifetime, and go
and have some fun.

FREE RANGE

Feather Down Farms, England

The Feather Down concept is a simple one. Guests, predominantly urban couples with young children and a vaguely eco-friendly consciousness, get back to nature on a small, working farm in a 'tented cottage'. We're talking canvas, but with wooden floors, real beds and duvets, and even a flushing loo – although there's no electricity or hot water. The farmer goes about his or her daily work, and guests can get involved, or enjoy the great outdoors in their own way.

Manor Farm in Hampshire, run by thirtysomethings Anna and Will Brock, is the first of ten Feather Down Farms planned around the UK. Ferrying our luggage in a wheelbarrow across the field, our tent, one of five, looked worryingly primitive. But inside it had a charming Little-House-on-the-Prairie-meets-Heidi vibe. A collection of unmatching wooden chairs sits around a huge table, and the focal point is a wood-burning stove. There's a sink, enamel crockery and glasses (no plastic here), framed photographs of cute animals straight from central casting, and a vintage toy or two, such as a small rocking horse.

Beds are in three sleeping areas: a double room (two singles pulled together), a room with bunks and a 'canopy bed' – a cupboard with mattress. The latter, with hinged doors and heart-shaped cut-outs, was a huge hit with the four children in our party, who rolled around in it like puppies. One side opens into the double room, so you won't just need your winceyette nightie because of the cold. And it can get cold, even in August.

When I showed a friend pictures of our 'tent', she said, 'Ha! I didn't think you'd cope with real camping'. And that was before I'd told her about Anna's Kitchen, an established business selling ready meals (we had excellent lamb tagine and beef stroganoff) made on the farm by Anna Brock. The other Feather Down Farms won't have a resident Anna, but all will have a twenty-four-hour honesty shop filled with local goodies, organic where possible, and basics like milk. But don't be misled by the food and Feather Down's cutesy good looks, because a stay here is surprisingly hard work.

You cook on top of a wood-burning stove that is easy to light but takes a while to get going. It also goes out overnight. Washing up is a nightmare in the tiny sink. And nights with real darkness are a shock to urbanites. Cooking, even with the help of Anna's Kitchen, took imagination, but I suppose it's these 'hardships' that make staying in a Feather Down Farm such a worthwhile experience. Basically, you're forced

Inside it had a charming Little-House-on-the-Prairie-meets-Heidi vibe

to relax into a slower pace of life, because there isn't any choice. When it takes an hour to make a cup of coffee, you appreciate drinking it all the more.

Get away from Nappy Valley

Getting into this way of thinking at the beginning is a fairly tortuous process, especially when you wake up in a freezing tent and aren't able to flick on a radiator or have a bath. But by the end you're more organised and try not to let the fire go out and, more importantly, you learn not to get so stressed about stupid things like the pasta taking an extra half hour to make. You also find yourself with more time on your hands, despite being busy keeping the fire stoked and endlessly hosing mud off the children.

Being on a real working farm, the children get to go semi-feral for a while. And, for a slummy mummy, it's fun to wear the same clothes day after day, not put on make up – a rare break from Nappy Valley of the Dolls where immaculate mums push equally immaculate children around all day.

I stayed with my sister-in-law (a first-time camper, who didn't find even the halfway house of a Feather Down experience the most relaxing holiday of her life), her seventeen-month-old son and his three male cousins aged seven to eleven. The children loved it, partly because the nanny state doesn't come into play here – if you're worried you might fall out of a tree, the ethos is not to go up there in the first place. They climbed on to enormous combine harvesters, were chased across a field by llama, and the little one fell face first into a dung-filled puddle (admittedly, he didn't like that bit much). The older boys churned up fields on hired bikes. Little girls in neighbouring tents made friends with the chickens and sheep housed in a pen in front of the tents and swung on rope swings. It was good old-fashioned fun.

The Feather Down Farm concept is idealistic, not necessarily for everyone and potentially a little too cold for comfort at the beginning and end of the season (take warm socks). You could even argue that this is camping for people who think they're too posh for caravans. But you return looking at your electric kettle in a new way, and proud at having 'survived'. And if survival means a real duvet, then I say carry on camping.

left and opposite **Fun down on the farm**

above **Even the washing up can seem like fun**

You could even argue that this is camping for people who think they're too posh for caravans

IDEAL AGE: 2–16

Manor Farm, West Worldham, Alton, Hampshire,
GU34 3BD, UK
Tel + 44 (0) 1420 80804
www.featherdownfarm.co.uk

There are also farms in Somerset, Cornwall,
Wiltshire, Herefordshire, Lincolnshire, Lancashire,
Warwickshire and Scotland. There are five tents
at each site. Accommodation is in tents sleeping
up to six people

Prices are per tent:
Weekends (Friday 4.00 p.m. – Monday 10.30 a.m.)
– from £195
Midweek (Monday 4.00 p.m. – Friday 10.30 a.m.)
– from £185
Week (Friday 4.00 p.m. – Friday 10.30 a.m.) – from £345
Rental of bed linen (sheet package) is an extra £5.75
per person

Excursions organised, bike rentals

MESSING ABOUT ON THE WATER

Canal Boating in England

'What happens if we crash?' were my first words to the Black Prince manager on seeing *Pippa*. There before me was a beautiful seventy-foot canal boat resplendent in black and maroon livery moored to the edge of a very narrow canal, and there behind me were six unruly children aged between seven and fourteen, one small dog and a fellow mother who was clearly harbouring the same reservations as me. 'No worries,' came the reassuring response, 'narrowboats take a bit of getting used to and everyone bangs them around a bit. Anyway, she's not wooden like you might think – her hull is made of steel.' Just as well I thought as the motley crew clambered aboard hauling suitcases and carrier bags of food for our adventure.

Crashing should have been the least of my concerns in those first few minutes. More pressing was the issue of turning *Pippa* around as, unfortunately, she was facing the wrong way. This was to be our first manoeuvre, carried out in full view of an experienced canal-boat fraternity, who watched in mild amusement at our complete incompetence.

Fortunately, the engineer who had taken us through a step-by-step guide to the workings of the boat, took pity on us and having turned us around, escorted us the first half-mile of the journey, safely guiding us through the first lock to a deserted point on the canal where, when left to our own devices, there'd be no tell-tale witnesses.

There are 3,000 miles of navigable waterways in the UK and countless places to begin and end a narrowboat holiday, according to which operator you select. Our base, at Stoke Prior in Worcestershire, is the headquarters of Black Prince, which specializes in the Midlands area and the 118 miles of canal linking Edinburgh and Glasgow. One week tends to be the average length of holiday, though enthusiasts can go for two, and those short of time or confidence (or both) can go for a three-day short break – the option we chose. Our humble ambition was to journey to Worcester, turn the boat at Digliss Docks – where the Worcester & Birmingham Canal meets the River Severn – and mosey on back the way we'd come, all in all a mere twenty-four-mile round trip.

If truth be told I had a number of misgivings about a canal-boat holiday. While the perfect environmentalist in me glowed at the thought of holidaying in the UK, the fair-weather sybarite warned of cramped conditions and torrential downpours. But somewhere, high in the heavens, the gods were smiling on us for we chanced upon three of those heart-stoppingly

There are 3,000 miles of navigable waterways in the UK and countless places to begin and end a narrow-boat holiday

above Working the locks on route

glorious days that make England and its countryside seem beautiful beyond compare. By day we lived outside, running barefoot along the towpath, picking blackberries from passing hedgerows, stopping for cold drinks at pubs along the route or lying spread-eagled in the sunshine on the roof of the boat; by night, as an eerie mist enveloped the canal, a full moon rose to lighten the depths of that rural darkness.

The laughter never stopped

And *Pippa*, too, exceeded all our expectations. While very large people (either upwards or outwards) might find the space restrictive, we fitted comfortably. Six of us shared three walk-through cabins with narrow beds, pillows and duvets, while the two eleven-year-old boys had sleeping bags and sofa beds. We had two

loos, a piping hot shower, a TV and CD player, and central heating. Even the kitchen, minute as it was, had a decent-sized cooker and fridge. The roof became our garden and the lock system our workout zone, where we pumped our biceps and strained our thighs through forty-four locks in three days.

Miraculously we survived without a mutiny from the children who, aside from lock work, were marshalled to various operational duties – driving the boat (even the seven-year-old had a go), mooring, dog-walking and washing-up. We crashed the boat repeatedly, though fortunately never into an oncoming barge, and we lost two children overboard at one stage. But the laughter never stopped.

So would I do a similar holiday again? The answer is a resounding yes, on the basis that journeying at less

than 5mph through towns and countryside, is a truly relaxing way to travel. Furthermore, the canals, towpaths, locks and bridges, so carefully maintained by British Waterways and the Inland Waterways Association, are in their best condition for 200 years. Now that the canals are no longer used commercially, they exist purely for the benefit of holidaymakers, ramblers and those who have made their homes on the water. But there is inevitably the weather issue. Would those fields and hedgerows have looked quite so appealing in driving rain? Probably not. Who would have elected to drive the boat from the al fresco steering point in the stern? Nobody. How would we have entertained all those children in a seven-foot wide space? With difficulty. But, if you're blessed with sunshine, you may just find it's more fun than you ever imagined.

Black Prince Holidays, Stoke Prior, Bromsgrove, Worcestershire B60 4LA, UK
Tel + 44 (0) 1527 575 115
www.black-prince.com

Black Prince Holidays are part of Drifters – a consortium of award-winning holiday boat companies (tel + 44 (0) 8457 626252; www.drifters.co.uk)
From £600 per boat for one week
£350 for a three- or four-day short break
Readers of *Heaven on Earth Kids* can enjoy the following discounts on Drifters holidays if they quote Castle Wharf Promotions/Heaven on Earth:
£50 off a part week
£100 off a full week
£250 off two weeks
This offer cannot be used in conjunction with any other offer

ANYONE FOR POLO?

Las Escobas, Argentina

With a broad smile and arms open wide, Pancho welcomes us to his family farm, Las Escobas, in the heart of the Argentine pampas. Angie, his elegant wife, smiles while offering refreshing cups of tea, and three children enthusiastically help with our luggage. Our quest for the perfect 'Argentine Polo Experience' has ended some 300 hot and dusty kilometres outside Buenos Aires under the blue dome of the sky in this vast warm landscape that was MADE to gallop across. And within hours that is exactly what we are doing – galloping into the setting sun. I want to holler, 'Yabba Dabba Dooooo!' like Fred Flintstone, and my son is grinning so broadly I think his face will split in two. Thundering across the pampas, hanging off the side of a horse, polo stick in hand – it just can't get much better than this.

Polo lovers from around the world flock to Las Escobas every year – amateurs, professionals, locals and novices alike, all making the regular pilgrimage to improve their skills with the help, instruction and guidance of six-goal player Pancho Marin-Moreno, because what Pancho doesn't know about polo just isn't worth knowing – from breeding a horse to selecting a saddle, fine tuning a shot or buying the right pair of *bombachas* (gaucho trousers, perfect for riding in).

The Moreno family has been prominent in the Argentine polo scene for three generations, with Pancho's father, the late Jorge Marin Moreno, winning the Queen's Cup and the Gold Cup many times. As Pancho says with his infectious broad smile, 'In my family, if you can breathe, you play polo'.

An athletic and confident horseman, Pancho spends half the year playing professional polo in England. For the other six months, he and his family are based at Las Escobas where Pancho the instructor and Angie the host welcome guests to the pampas for a few weeks to learn polo or improve their game with the help of Pancho's resident professionals (all three- and five-goal players).

Our high-spirited sunset ride gives Pancho the chance to assess our standard of play, and later we are asked to select from forty ponies, five that will become our own 'string of five' during our time at Las Escobas. Among others I am encouraged to pick Mammoth – I glance at my own inappropriately sized girth and wonder if this is a hint – perhaps not, as Gorda (Fat One) is pushed towards the slimmest and trimmest member of our group. Who will get El Pescado (The Fish)? My son gets Mugre, it means 'dirt', but the horse should be called the 'Clever One'.

Thundering across the pampas, hanging off the side of a horse, polo stick in hand

Mugre has an annual conflict with Don Louis, one of the elder grooms. All year they both wait patiently for the fruit to ripen on one particularly delicious pear tree in the garden. It is usually Don Louis who loses out, 'Ee gets SO cross, the orse was standing on ees two feet, climbing the tree, ee looks like a giraffe, getting all the pears that are ripe!' Another story punctuated with that broad smile.

Excitement beyond measure

For two or three weeks (you can decide how long you want to stay) the daily routine starts with Angie's breakfast, which includes fruits picked from trees in the garden or from nearby woods. Stick and ball practice follows, with many changes of horse; Pancho giving continuous encouragement and, being a gifted teacher, is not shy of handing out the occasional well-deserved bollocking. You will practice forehand, backhand, nearside, offside, under-neck shots, hooking your opponents stick and 'riding off' – described by my son as a 'mounted rugby tackle'. And just when you think your body can take no more, you find yourself back at the farm, jumping in the pool, wolfing down lunch and grabbing that all-important siesta.

Re-grouping mid-afternoon with a cup of tea or even some *matté* (a green tea exclusive to South America), Pancho hands out tactical advice and gives a quick de-brief on the morning session before we are all back on our ponies for an afternoon chukka with the resident professionals. And this is what we are all here for – the thundering hooves, sheer adrenalin, man and beast, the blur of the landscape, trying to hit that small white ball, with seven other horses and riders doing the same thing – excitement beyond measure. We carry on till the sun sinks lower, and the whole pampas becomes bathed in a golden light. As we amble home, ponies exhausted, Pancho still has the energy to share his love and knowledge of the Argentine countryside, pointing out and admiring a whole variety of birds, rare plants, angry insects and summer flowers along our path. 'Tomorrow we'll go armadillo hunting' he promises with a smile.

During your time at the farm you might be lucky enough to find yourself playing in a local tournament, family versus family, followed by an all-night *asado* (barbeque). This is polo like you have never imagined. One year, when no local opposition was on offer, Pancho organised a Battle of the Sexes, a brave thing

Thundering hooves, sheer adrenalin, man and beast, the blur of the landscape

to do in Argentina. 'NEVER AGAIN', the smile absent for once, 'A big mistake – the fighting! – I say to them, "Hey, hey, hey, we are all friends here, yes?" NAH – Never again.' The smile returns to his face

Angie welcomes us back home, and the laughter and the stories continue flying across the table as we hungrily devour her dinner by candlelight, before there is an unseemly scramble to get into bed before the generator is switched off, plunging the house into total darkness.

Hot Dog

The house is the centre of this working *estancia*. It is a functional house, simple and rustic, gently touched by Angie's femininity, but filled every evening with the scent of the honeysuckle planted when she first came here. In the cool dark drawing room polo is in evidence in ever corner, a line of trophies dating as

far back as 1968, fading photographs of handsome champions, a helmet swinging from a chair, framed newspaper cuttings turning sepia. The more recent trophies gleam, and familiar names like Cartier, Cirencester and Cowdray Park are engraved on everything from clocks to cups, photograph frames and statues, each representing another victory for Las Escobas.

But it's not all work and no play – Oh no! – Pancho is a nickname and it means 'Hot Dog', and this is one Hot Dog that likes to party – be it in London, Buenos Aires or Pergamino. There are many stories of nights out in Pergamino, the local town, thirty kilometres away, stories that invariably end up with either a guest or a resident professional lurching home from ditch to ditch, and not always making the morning lesson – stories that need not be repeated here. But it was on one of those wild nights many years ago that the then bachelor Pancho was looking for some

English speaking girls to help him with his guests, when he was introduced to the lovely Angie. 'This girl is far too good for the English – I'll keep her for myself,' thought Pancho. It took him a few years, but eventually Angie agreed to marry her attractive polo player – and the wait was well worth it – they are a powerful team, and with their three charming children following them around the world the envy of many.

'I am so happy here' smiles Pancho. I too, am so happy here. Riding home this evening from the lower practice field, sun gently setting, I watched Tommy, Pancho's young son herding a few head of cattle with my own son – their evident pleasure was priceless. Pancho keeps these cattle just so that his children can enjoy 'being a cowboy for a day'. Now THAT is a love and understanding of the pampas, its wildlife and all that it has to offer.

The laughter
and the stories
continue flying
across the table

IDEAL AGE: 8–16

Pancho and Angie Marin Moreno, Las Escobas, Pergamino, Buenos Aires, Argentina
Tel +54 2477 490025 (Las Escobas) or +44 (0) 118 930 573

Rates from US$250 per day for horses, instruction, room and board

LAND OF THE OSCARS

Touring in New Zealand

Two key facts about Kiwi country shaped the general plan when my family – which included Mum, Dad, daughters aged thirteen and eleven and son aged four – set off for our holiday of a lifetime. Number one, since New Zealand is about as far as you can go, we decided to break the journey on the way out. And secondly, since the country is as big as Britain, we rejected the idea of a head to toe approach, opting instead to spend most of our two weeks just in the North Island.

After a twelve-hour flight we soft landed in Singapore. The transfer from immigration at Changi airport, where each desk had a little bowl of boiled sweets for tiny tired fingers, to the Shangri-La hotel, took less than thirty minutes. We checked in, threw off our clothes and dived straight into the enormous pool where we floated on our backs, embalmed in warmth, and fell in love with the night sky and the shushing of the palm fronds. We had arrived. Well, halfway at least.

Our photo album tells all: Kids eating with their fingers off banana leaves in Little India (all those 'use your knife and fork properly' nags gone in a flash of exotic fun), riding the cable car to the island of Sentosa, stroking dolphins, and the parrot in the Jurong Birdpark who sang – believe me, I was there – 'Happy Birthday' to Francesca (her fourteenth). For higher education we visited the excellent Heritage Centre in Chinatown, vividly showing the tough times of early settlers, and took the absolutely unmissable night safari where nocturnal animals go about their business in a setting that feels more like an Amazonian rainforest than a zoo. But it was soon time to move on.

Winging down to Wellington

No boiled sweets this time but a special channel at immigration just for families with children. We picked up a hired people carrier and in less than fifteen minutes from the airport we were in our four-room guesthouse in the waterfront suburb of Seatoun. The scenery was as wild as western Scotland, yet we were only a few minutes from the middle of New Zealand's capital.

Wellington has the buzz of a cosmopolitan, lifestyle city but the intimacy of a small town, all tightly packaged on the waterfront in a horseshoe of green hills. Our prime site was Te Papa, a celebration of all things NZ and a good place to begin any trip to the country. It's far more than a museum. As well as being a repository of national treasures, this iconic work of architecture is full of surprises, from Maori 'haka' ceremonial welcomes staged in a mock wooden

The scenery was as wild as western Scotland, yet only a few minutes from the middle of New Zealand's capital

'marae' community house, to virtual bungee jumping and imaginative shows of the awesome forces that shaped all those Tolkien landscapes.

If locations were awarded Oscars, New Zealand would have its sideboard groaning with them. As soon as you drive anywhere you see what the fuss is about. Think of any landscape and you'll find it here in this world-in-one-country, and all the more impressive in the flesh than any digitally enhanced, specially-effected screen portrayal. And not only is the scenery outrageous but with only four million people in a country the same size as ours, the roads seem empty.

Our five-hour drive to Lake Taupo was broken by a stop to walk on the big beach of Otaki and lunch in the garden at the delightful Brown Sugar Café in tiny Taihape. We also had our first encounter with Middle Earth in the shape of the trio of volcanoes at Tongariro, the world's second largest national park (after Yellowstone in the US).

Lake Taupo, according to a local fishing guide, has some of the best wild trout fishing in the world, 'some so big that you'll be able to see the water level drop when you catch one.' Formed just 2,000 years ago, in an eruption so cataclysmic that the sun went hazy over China from the dusting, Taupo has become a mecca for sporties; from fishing to bungee jumping, rafting to skydiving.

We left the fishing for fissures, following the Thermal Explorer Highway past hillsides still venting their fiery tempers with plumes of steam, to Rotorua, a primeval soup kitchen of bubbling cauldrons and wild stinky geysers, an incandescent world still in the making.

Onwards and upwards – maybe five hours in all – to the Coromandel Peninsula, through landscapes as lush in parts as the Caribbean, in others more like natural parklands that could pass as Capability Brown creations. We stayed at the surfing seaside of Whangamata, checking into one of three garden cottages that make

up the delightful Brenton Lodge before hitting the high street, renting wetsuits and boogie boards from ex-world champion Dean Williams' shop on Port Road and casting off into the gentle surf on its fabulous beach. Two girls became instant converts to Surf Culture, with terrifying cost implications.

Late-life crisis

Auckland, which spreads as wide as LA, has sea on all flanks and a bay full of boats. Just as *Lord of the Rings* put New Zealand's landscapes under the global spotlight, so the 2002 America's Cup did for Auckland's waters. You can boat the bay on a variety of craft, most of which leave from the happening waterfront. We picked *NZL40*, built for the 1995 America's Cup and the maritime equivalent to a Formula One racing car, stripped to the barest of hulls and a sky-scraping hundred-foot-high mainsail. We all had turns at the wheel, racing around the harbour at awesome speeds. We also took the lift 700 feet up to the top of the Sky Tower, the tallest structure south of the Equator, to see who would dare walk on the alarming glass-floored viewing gallery. The panoramic windows are filled not only with views but also with the occasional Kiwi preparing to plummet to earth harnessed to a cable above.

We explored various parts, including the preserved Victorian boutique village of Parnell, the more alternative Ponsonby and the maritime suburb of Birkenhead, a ferry hop across the harbour. And we also hopped on the thirty-minute ferry to Waiheke, a gorgeous toy town island in the middle of the Hauraki Gulf and a wonderful world of beaches, forests, farmland and boutique vineyards, Stony Ridge among them. It was right here that I went through my late-life crisis.

We were in a park, beside a beach, children at play, boats in the water. In less than an hour we would be driving to the airport for the first leg of the long journey home. I suddenly had a terrible feeling that

If locations were awarded Oscars, New Zealand would have its sideboard groaning with them

I'd missed the whole point of living. Our home should have been here, living a life of greens and blues and boats and beaches and seafood and sauvignons and walks and wilderness. I simply didn't want to go home. And therein lies both the pleasure and pain of New Zealand. You don't so much go for a holiday but to sample a way of life. And if, like us, you have a fantastic time, the prospect of returning to Britain can be deeply saddening. All air tickets should carry a health warning.

above **Lake Taupo serenity**
opposite **Rotorua's fiery temper explodes**

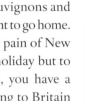

IDEAL AGE: 6–16

For further details contact Bridge & Wickers,
3 The Courtyard, 44 Gloucester Avenue,
Primrose Hill, London NW1 8JD, UK
Tel +44 (0) 20 7483 6555
www.bridgeandwickers.co.uk

Bridge & Wickers are specialists in experience-led holidays throughout New Zealand

TWO PERFECT WEEKS

Touring in Australia

It's almost as far as you can go, and gargantuan when you get there (thirty times bigger than the UK and a five-hour flight just from one end to the other). Yet, according to the tourist board, Australia, the ultimate dream destination, is well worth the trip even if you've only got two weeks – which is just as well since that's all that many families can take.

But how can you avoid the classic Down Under Blunder of trying to pack everything into one visit? With careful planning and pruning. Here's a blueprint, as recorded in real time, of a first-hand, two-week trip during our winter (their summer!).

The seaside

First the bad news, but you'll soon get over it. You not only tie up twenty-four hours of your holiday getting there but you lose eleven hours in time zones in the process. If you go after work on Friday night you'll get there at dawn on Sunday. Saturday never really happens. It gets lost in transit.

However, there's no better place in the world to convalesce from faraway flying than an Australian beach. They are among the best in the world. If you fly straight into Brisbane you could, in just a two-hour drive south, reach Byron Bay, a low rise, laid back and beach-gorgeous resort. Check into your hotel, drop your bags and britches on the floor, slip on the swimmers and hit the surf. You'll be born again.

Byron Bay is a perfect seaside for a perfect few days in a perfect two weeks Down Under. As a work of nature, it is stunning. It sits at one end of a forty kilometre-long, wrap-around beach backed by a horseshoe of purple-hazed mountain ridges, all part of a massive volcanic caldera that blew its top twenty million years ago. The sands are so fine they squeak underfoot, the sea is a flotsam of surfers, swimmers and sea-kayakers. And such is the forgiving surf that both children and parents can learn to surf their socks off, with lessons easily arranged on the spot.

The coast drive

There are more than 500 miles of Pacific Coast Highway One between you and Sydney, more if you are tempted by sideroads that line up like teeth on a comb and lead to deserted beaches. The passing road cuts through a variety of scenery, from swampy bayou country and acres of whispering sugar cane, thick forests of gum trees and mountain slopes that tumble into the sea wearing a coat of bananas. Such is the

The sands are so fine they squeak underfoot, the sea is a flotsam of surfers, swimmers and sea-kayakers

Sun, sand, surfing and kangaroo cuddles

variety of en route distractions that you'll very rarely suffer those 'when are we going to get there' groans from the back seat. Especially with a couple of interesting stops along the way.

Make Coffs Harbour your first break and stay at the Novotel Pacific Bay, which has a kids' club as well as pools, tennis and a beach. Don't miss, in fact you can't miss, the Big Banana, a 'horticultural theme park' with a huge great concrete banana over the entrance. And your second port of call should be Port Stephens where you can join a dolphin-spotting boat trip on the deep bite of sheltered water, as well as take a walk through the Tilligery Peninsula national park. It's home to a community of koalas who sit in the high branches on the lookout for British families and bordered by surf-pounded wild beaches.

Instead of sticking to the Pacific Highway, which would have you in Sydney from Port Stephens is less than three hours, spend the day slowly looping through the Hunter Valley, Australia's oldest wine growing district. Of course, Australian top drops will hold little interest to children but they'll be welcome in most of the estates, although they'll have to forgo the tastings. You could also detour to Barrington Tops for a bit of kangaroo spotting.

The city

The anticipation you feel as you approach Sydney for the first time is buttock clenching, the last few miles – through thick forests, national park and across the Hawkesbury River is an incredible show of nature. But nothing can prepare you for the final leap across the Harbour Bridge with the Opera House to port, the iconic masterpiece of this fabulous city captured in a single frame. There should be a warning sign, 'Drivers, keep your eyes on the road!'

Iconic Sydney harbour

Such is its knockout stock of holiday essentials that you could spend a perfect two weeks Down Under just in Sydney. The menu includes around thirty beaches, from wild and surfy to soup-bowl calm and toddler friendly. A national park lies right in its heart as well as a botanic garden where laughing kooka-burras, long-snouted ibis, cockatoos, screaming mynahs and fruit bats the size of rugby balls share the exotic subtropical canopy. Sydney is a city of world-class museums, boat trips, shops selling surfwear (a teenage girl's heaven), quirky neighbour-hoods, street markets and hotels with – not to be underestimated for convenience and cost-saving – full kitchen facilities.

From Sydney it's home, arriving as the cock crows the next morning, so have a thick sweater handy. The good news is that you get to make up all those time zones you lost in getting there.

You could
spend a perfect
two weeks
Down Under
just in Sydney

IDEAL AGE: 6–16

For further details contact Bridge & Wickers,
3 The Courtyard, 44 Gloucester Avenue,
Primrose Hill, London NW1 8JD, UK
Tel +44 (0) 20 7483 6555
www.bridgeandwickers.co.uk

Bridge & Wickers are specialists in experience-led holidays throughout Australia

CULTURE KIDS

Prague, Czech Republic

City breaks can be hard work with kids. We baked in Rome and had a hard time prising our two away from the pool in order to look at Signor Bernini's statues. That said, my teenage son was blown away by the interior of his first baroque church. We really hadn't been expecting that as parents, and it was a godsend, something that bridged the gap between our desire to catch up on European culture and the wall of adolescent torpor we were encountering at the time.

Architecture can be a good way to introduce children to art. A lot of art forms need explanation. Sculpture, opera, and poetry don't always communicate directly, but architecture is so accessible. You only have to enter a building to become part of 'the dialogue'. Not that I put it like that last week in Prague. I'd no wish to have my offspring tell me I was disappearing up my own bottom. We'd gone for a weekend break and I thought John would be excited seeing what is in fact a whole baroque new town built on the banks of the Vltava. We have the Thirty Years' War to thank for the fact that the Czech capital was rebuilt in Catholicism's florid new style, but John couldn't care less. Rome was two years ago. 'Frankly Dad, I've had enough serpentine columns.'

It was like taking a child to Disney only to find they no longer care for Mickey. Once we'd done the astronomical clock, visited the shop that sells reproduction armour and decided against the Museum of Sex Machines, what on earth was there to do? I was certainly not going to pay for endless ice creams.

The quest for art nouveau

Then, thank goodness, we saw Storch House whose whole frontage disappears under a welter of intricate painting known as sgraffito. 'Who's that?' asked Livvie pointing to a figure.

'Er, Good King Wenceslas,' I replied, checking with my guidebook.

'He looks like a woman.'

'Ah well,' I bluffed. 'People did in those days.'

The image was by a man called Mikulas Ales. It was very soulful, very Alfons Mucha, as were the life-size artisans depicted nearby on the shop front of Rott's. The Czechs have been painting the fronts of their houses since the Middle Ages but when art nouveau erupted at the end of the nineteenth century, as a national statement, they redecorated many of their older buildings in Mucha's limpid new style.

Architecture can be a good way to introduce children to art

By the time we were entering the Jewish quarter John and Liv had developed a game of 'Spot the Sad Lady'. On the front of a house in Parizska they discovered the Sad Lady had developed three dimensions and very large breasts. She was also holding up the lintel of a merchant's front door. At the Grand Hotel Europa they found her with two friends, all gilded, disporting themselves on top of the elaborate hotel signage.

'Why do they write the names up in gold?' John asked. It was true – we'd now seen three hotels spelled out in big gold capitals and on the top of the Praha House PRAHA was formed in gold letters that stretched ingeniously round the windows of the top floor.

'Well, art nouveau was a very celebratory style,' I said.

'What's art nouveau?'

I kept my head down at that point. 'I know, let's try and find some stone foliage and semi-circular stained glass over doorways!'

'Why?' My son asked.

'First one to spot some gets an ice cream.'

Big boobies

It was a good afternoon. We took in the spectacular Hotel Central that has plasterwork tree branches all the way up its façade, and Hlavni Nadrazi, the main railway station, which has lots of curvy metalwork and huge naked statues (male and female) holding up the inaugural plaque. That brought forth titters, of course. Liv also thought it funny that the architect, Josef Fanta, shared his name with John's favourite drink.

Prague has two kinds of art nouveau – that which was imposed sgraffito-style on earlier buildings – and the real thing like the glorious Municipal House where we had tea. I kept quiet about the fact that my guidebook claimed this as one of the best art nouveau buildings in middle Europe, but when we peeped into the mayoral salon and saw gilded Sad Ladies on the top of every column it was a bit obvious that a theme was developing.

'I bet there's a lady with Big Boobies somewhere around here,' Livvie announced. It took us a while to find her but yes there she was in a semi-circular mosaic over the front of the Municipal Building, sidling up to a rather distracted looking king.

'Why's she naked?' John asked.

I improvised 'It's symbolic.'

'What of?'

It was a good question. Truth? Purity? The advantages of being king? My guidebook was silent on the subject.

'At the time people just liked putting naked women on public buildings,' I suggested. 'And they wanted to make them look real rather than idealised.'

'Why?'

'It was all to do with celebrating the people of the country. In some places the style was known as National Romantic.'

'What style?'

'Art nouveau.' There, I'd said it again.

'OK,' they said. The label wasn't so frightening now. Now it was fun. In Male Namesti the two of them almost came to blows over whether the black and white sgraffito on a mediaeval house was art nouveau or not.

'There are naked ladies,' said John.

'But they're in black and white,' Liv insisted.

'So – they didn't have colour film in those days.'

Well, I think the message got through on some level.

IDEAL AGE: 11–16

For details of family-friendly breaks in Prague contact Holidays from Heaven

Tel + 44 (0) 118 933 3777

www.holidaysfromheaven.com

TIPS

European Cultural Breaks With The Family

- Stay somewhere central. Hours on public transport go down badly
- Interweave looking at culture with familiar activities – toyshops, McDonalds, ice cream parlours
- Try and make it seem fun. Never use the words 'But this is good for you'
- Using guilt, 'When I was your age I would have given my eye teeth to come somewhere like this' won't work. No one ever enjoys themselves out of a sense of obligation. You'll also get asked what eye teeth are

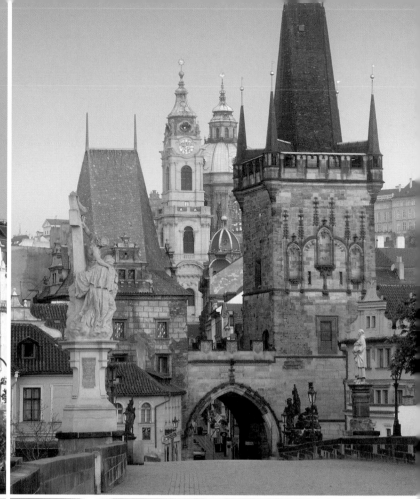

MAD ABOUT MICKEY

Disneyland Paris, France

To be honest, the question on my mind was, 'Is it really worth visiting?' Moreover, could the reality of the much-maligned Disneyland Paris possibly live up to the fantasy images first created by Walt Disney over seventy years ago? The brochure looked plasticy and flavourless; a sort of tourism laced with the visual equivalent of entertainment E-numbers.

Children, on the other hand, are immediately susceptible to glitzy colour and totally enchanted by the concept of the universal dream-come-trueness proffered by the Disney pleasure dome – walking around in wonderment of everything that befalls their wide-eyed stares.

Some of their excitement must have seeped through our disbelieving skins because as soon as we glimpsed the iconic pink turrets of Sleeping Beauty's castle all hesitancy vanished and we were instantly transformed into gleeful pleasure seekers bitten by the Disney bug.

Situated thirty-two kilometres east of Paris, Disney's first foray on European soil opened in 1992. After a rocky start, it made it to the top of the heap to become Europe's number one tourist attraction. And what it lacks in culture it makes up for in fun. All the classic original Disney attractions are present in updated Francocised models including: 'It's a Small World', 'Pirates of the Caribbean' and the ever-popular 'Big Thunder Mountain'. Queuing was vastly reduced with the free FastPass system available on the most popular attractions, allowing us to return to the ride later in the day. Even better, we sent one person in our group ahead with everyone's admission tickets to save traipsing around together.

Encompassing a site of nearly twenty square kilometres, it is divided into three clear areas of distinctly different activities: the Walt Disney Studios (think lights, cameras, action); the Disneyland Park (think funfair); and the Disney Village (for retail therapy and eateries). The Park is both the largest and main attraction, with themed zones offering non-stop Adventure, Discovery and Fantasy. Allow at least three whole days if you want to cover everything.

Each area has a subtle combination of big thrills for those who bliss out on sensory overload, and family adventures suitable for all ages. While you can never be too old or too young to visit, if you're looking for the right moment to go it's worth noting that some rides have a height restriction for children under 140cm.

Buffalo Bill's Wild West Show provided a rousing start to our weekend. While the audience dined out

We were instantly transformed into gleeful pleasure seekers bitten by the Disney bug

on spare ribs and chilli, bare-chested Indians and cowboys on galloping horses cavorted around the arena herding full-blooded bulls and stampeding bison, all to the rhythm of patriotic hillbilly anthems. You don't get that in the West End.

Following the screams

Early in the Park the following morning, we stood debating where to start. 'Let's go where the screams are' said one daughter. Off we headed to Space Mountain ('the most sophisticated state-of-the-art adventure of its kind in the world, in homage to French visionary Jules Verne', said the guidebook). As the cannon pounded and recoiled under the green and brass dome, shafts of fluorescent light appeared through the jets of steam. Ten seconds later the rocket fired, launching twenty-four screaming passengers through the barrel to the summit in 1.8 seconds. After a second of zero gravity, we descended, at high speed, into the black depths of outer space passing planets and narrowly missing flaming comets. 'I never knew it could be this much fun', said my husband.

From one ride to another, we eagerly explored the areas, barely tiring and losing all track of time. We were almost tempted not to bother with the Studios. However, that would have been a big mistake. From action packed car chases and motorbike stunts in the 'Lights!, Moteurs!, Action' stunt show to 'Cinemagique' in Studio Two, which creatively depicted the history of moving pictures in a very (I don't want to spoil it for you) experiential way.

The finale of the second day was the 'Rock 'N' Roller' coaster, spitting us out from nought to 100kph in less than three seconds before looping the loop in pitch black to the sound of heavy rock. And so it went on.

Accommodation comes in various guises. Nearest to the theme parks is the Disneyland Hotel and if nothing but the best will do then this is the one to book. However, if you're happy to walk for a few minutes or take a very short bus ride then other options include: the Hotel New York with funky themed Parkside diner, deco swimming pool and ice rink (in the winter months); the highly recommended Newport Bay Club; the Chip and Dale themed Sequoia Lodge; the ingeniously designed Hotel Cheyenne resembling a Wild

opposite **Drenching at Big Thunder Mountain**
above **Excitement at Buffalo Bill's Wild West show**

We stood debating where to start. 'Let's go where the screams are' said one daughter

above **Pirates of the Caribbean** opposite (clockwise from top left) **Space Mountain terror: ground to summit in 1.8 seconds; the locals greet you wherever you are; Pinocchio leads the parade; Lights! Moteurs! Action! stuntshow**

West town; the budget-priced Santa Fe; and the rustic Davy Crockett Ranch where families sleep in log cabins and can enjoy additional outdoor activities.

Dinner at Inventions in the 'Fantasia' restaurant of the Disneyland Hotel is an essential highlight. A deliciously healthy spread in the company of Mini Mouse in her clompy yellow trotters, the long-tongued Pluto, seven-foot Goofy and friendly Pinocchio, was the perfect end to an action packed day.

There are fast food outlets everywhere with names like Cowboy Cookout and Pizza Planet and a few notable restaurants. The Blue Lagoon, adjacent to the popular Pirates of the Caribbean, specialises in seafood recipes – we enjoyed couscous and red snapper.

Our youngest daughter summed up her stay so completely we couldn't argue. 'Can I do one more ride Mummy?', she said. 'Oh yes, which one?' I questioned. 'The go to bed ride,' she replied.

Needless to say, we organised a FastPass.

IDEAL AGE: 5–65

TIPS

- Get a FastPass to avoid unnecessary queues
- Ask the concierge to make lunch and dinner reservations or you'll risk missing a sit-down meal in the restaurant of your choice
- Take a rucksack of healthy snacks and drinks to keep going – you'll be walking all day and it can be quite hard going
- Visit off peak (January–March, May–June, October–November) to avoid the largest crowds

Disneyland Resort Paris, Marne La Vallée, Cedex 04, Paris, France
Tel + 44 (0) 8705 030303
www.disneylandparis.com

Open 365 days a year from 9.00 a.m. – 6.00 p.m.
(8.00 p.m. weekends and 11.00 p.m. in July and August)
Prices vary depending on hotel and time of year
Rooms are designed for between one and four people

ANIMAL MAGIC

Disney World, Florida, USA

If you have children then at some point or another you will probably face the prospect of a trip of Disney World in Florida. Opened in 1971 the world's biggest pleasure park resort is impossible to ignore. Four theme parks, water parks, golf courses, a sports complex, hotels galore and all in the glorious Florida sunshine give it mega pulling power in the holiday stakes.

The sheer number of attractions on offer mean that a family can spend as much or as little time there as they want, and anything from a weekend break to a two-week stay can be made to work for you. Perhaps the most educationally relevant of the theme parks is the Animal Kingdom, based around the notion of animal conservation. Cleverly linking Disney films, such as *Pochahontas*, *A Bug's Life*, *The Lion King* and *Finding Nemo* to the ideas of natural balance, harmony and animal survival, the park features spectacular rides, shows, jungle treks, interactive games and everything else you would expect from Disney. Our favourite was the Kilimanjaro Safari.

'Hi everyone and welcome to our photographic safari,' chirped Stephanie. 'I'll be your driver for the next two weeks and we're going to have a great time!'

'Stop pulling that silly face,' my stepdaughter whispered.

I must admit I was a bit wary of safari Disney-style. The Animal Kingdom may have imported all the animals we'd encountered on a real safari in Tanzania but I was dubious about the element of play-acting common to all Disney rides.

Convincing landscapes

I watched as Stephanie guided our game vehicle expertly on to rails as we crossed the bridge out of Harambe town. Suddenly we lurched alarmingly as the bridge 'swayed' and almost collapsed. The idea was to give us a cleverly manufactured frisson of the bridge being unsafe – which, of course, it wasn't. Everything in Disney is so safe you sometimes long for Goofy to do something unscripted. That's one of my problems with Disney. Last night in the Magic Kingdom we'd sat down at the only Italian restaurant in the world not to serve wine. 'I'm sorry sir, this is a dry Kingdom,' chirped the waitress.

That said, the landscape through which Stephanie 'drove' us was pretty convincing and so were the animals. There was a creek with real crocs, a pool with real hippos and reticulated giraffe that

The sheer number of attractions on offer mean that a family can spend as much or as little time there as they want

only looked animatronic because giraffes do move in a slo-mo animatronic way.

'Do keep a look out for black rhino,' calls out Stephanie on the PA and we knew fairly soon that we were going to see one right round the next corner. Indeed we did, and then up on a rock to our left we saw a splendidly maned lion pacing up and down. 'Wow, quite rare to see them about,' says Stephanie. Well, no, not really. With a big drop on all sides of this plateau, once the King Lion has been installed in the morning he ain't going nowhere till keepers from the Animal Kingdom come and collect him for the night.

Nevertheless Livvie enjoyed it hugely and I have to admit that Disney has edited out the dull bits – which can run into hours and hours on a real safari as you travel miles down hot dusty roads to see nothing more exciting than a rather confused looking wildebeest which then bolts as soon as he's in camera range.

Hang on everybody!

Just as I was getting reconciled to zebras on demand, Stephanie received a 'message' from Wilson, the park warden, up in his spotter plane (allegedly). 'There are poachers in the area! Can we help?' 'Oh no,' cried Stephanie as we turned a corner and found the poachers' camp with the fire still smoking and a recently abandoned pile of tusks. 'Hang on everybody!'

I'm not quite certain what happened next but we drove at speed around a series of bumpy bends and managed to cut off the poachers from their escape route, and somehow rescued a baby elephant. The next thing I knew we'd turned yet another corner to see Little Red, the really animatronic baby elephant, and Wilson, the equally fake park warden, triumphant together. Wilson had landed his plane, loaded the baby into a crate and seemed to be waving from the cockpit with a fixed smile on his face. 'I think Wilson's dead and the poachers are working his arm,' I whispered to my wife. But Livvie was waving back. She'd just saved Little Red.

'Well,' said Stephanie. 'We're going to have to cut our safari a bit short!' In fact we'd had less than thirty minutes of it by my reckoning. But that didn't matter. I'd only paid seventy dollars for the whole expedition (theme park included), not the thousands it would have cost to get to the real Serengeti. And we'd seen plenty of animals. My stepdaughter had even been an eco-hero. You can't really complain.

Up on a rock to our left we saw a splendidly maned lion pacing up and down

IDEAL AGE: 5–65

Disney's Animal Kingdom Lodge, Walt Disney World, Florida, USA
Tel +1 (407) 938 3000
www.disneyworld.com

Double rooms from US$240
One day, one theme park ticket US$71.36

above **Kilimanjaro Safari**
opposite **Animal magic at Animal Kingdom**

SHOPPING AND THE CITY

New York, USA

Turning ten, or 'double figs' as my grandmother used to call it, is a symbolic moment in the life of a child. I've always told my children that for their tenth birthdays they would be treated to their first overseas adventure. My eldest son was given a narrow selection of destinations from which to choose including the Pyramids at Giza, the Colosseum in Rome and Mount Etna (he was mad about volcanoes at the time). He chose none of them, deciding instead he'd rather travel by train than plane – not altogether surprising as the Twin Towers had just come crashing down. We went to Paris instead, by Eurostar, and had two lovely days zooming from the Sacre Coeur to Notre Dame, from Les Invalides to the Eiffel Tower and feasting between times on *steak frites* and *croque monsieur*.

My daughter, Polly, proved a little more wily when it came to her turn – probably because she'd had a good two years to plan her campaign. By that stage, too, we'd clocked up both Rome and Egypt as family holidays so she knew she'd be able to throw the net a little wider. When the moment came for me to ask her where she wanted to go, there was no hesitation. 'New York, please Mummy.' As simple as that.

New York might not be every ten-year-old's cup of tea but for a girl who has lived all her life in London, watched far too much television and grown up in a post 9/11 world peppered with images of that fateful day, Manhattan seemed like the centre of the universe.

We decided to do it in style, and true style in New York means only one thing – a suite at the Four Seasons, from the windows of which, thirty-two floors up, we could survey the serried ranks of one skyscraper after the next, peep through the gaps to Central Park and peer down from on high at the toy town of taxis and people far beneath us.

A good head for heights

As a vertigo sufferer, Polly has never had much time for tall buildings, yet if ever there was a city where you need a good head for heights it's New York. And first stop, like the good tourists we were, was the Empire State Building. The first tip here is to buy your tickets on-line in advance which means that once passed the initial security-check queue (be warned, it often snakes round the block outside) you are fast-tracked up the building. And the second tip is to rent an audio headset at the top which takes you through a 360-degree tour of all the landmark buildings on Manhattan Island and explains the city's logical grid-system layout. Thereafter New York is your oyster.

Thirty-two floors up, we could survey the serried ranks of one skyscraper after the next

With glee we fell into one tourist trap after another – a ride round Central Park in a horse and carriage, a memorable show on Broadway, a zoom round the Rockefeller Centre and an evening trip to the neon-lit Times Square. Philistines that we are, we eschewed all museums and went shopping instead – to Bloomingdales for the Little Brown Bag, to Dylan's Candy Bar for a thousand sweets and to Serendipity for a frozen hot chocolate ice cream. We never made it to Liberty Island – we ran out of time – and neither did we do the famous helicopter ride over the city (there must be limits to how much fun a child can have all in one go).

And then, of course, we went to Ground Zero – a moment of sobriety in a trip of incalculable pleasure and indulgence. But its significance was hard to fathom for a ten-year-old brain and try as she might she couldn't equate that empty space with those two famous towers.

In our two days there, we walked the streets till our shoes wore thin. Police sirens wailed, the manhole covers oozed steam, the American flag fluttered everywhere and billboards touted an endless array of lifestyle must-haves. It was just like the movies, just like the New York we hoped it would be and just the kind of trip I'd like to do every year with my gorgeous girl.

Just before we left for the airport an old friend of mine came to meet us for coffee in the hotel. She asked Polly what she thought of the city now that it was time to go home. 'My life began when I came to New York,' came the unabashed response that had me diving into my bag for our passports and tickets. 'I think one day I'd like to live here,' she added. And if she ever does, I'll be right there with her.

opposite **The Chrysler building and Times Square**   above **Central Park**
right **Shopping in style on Fifth Avenue**

IDEAL AGE: 10–16

Four Seasons Hotel, 57 East 57th Street, New York, New York 10022, USA
Tel + 1 (212) 758 5700
www.fourseasons.com/newyork

364 rooms
Double rooms from US$595

KING OF THE KASBAH

Climbing in Morocco

It is sometime just after dawn and I'm standing on the summit of a 14,000-foot mountain watching the surrounding peaks shift in colour from shady grey, through rose pink to golden brown as the sun rises higher in the sky. The air is thin and cold and my head is throbbing slightly from lack of oxygen, but the view is incredible. Looking one way I can see the vast emptiness of the Sahara stretching to the horizon; looking the other, beneath a thin veil of early morning cloud, are the plains of Marrakesh. Beside me my thirteen-year-old son, who has just completed the longest walk of his life, is wearing a slightly pained expression from altitude and exhaustion that suggests we should probably start our descent sooner rather than later.

Our adventure together started two days ago when, having picked up my son from school, we caught a flight to Morocco. We had decided several months before that a holiday together would be good, but a challenge would be even better. He's a strong boy and a good walker whose love of the mountains, shared with mine, is rooted in long summer holidays spent tramping through Snowdonia. Europe's biggest mountains are fairly technical even in the summer months and we wanted height without the crampons or the ropes. Where better, therefore, than the Atlas Mountains,

whose dusty, barren heights make perfect walking territory? And why not Jbel Toubkal – the highest in the range and the highest in North Africa?

After a night in Marrakesh and a morning exploring the souk we took a four-wheel-drive transfer to the mountains, our destination was the small village of Imlil above which, on a rocky promontory stands the Kasbah du Toubkal. The Kasbah, a rustic but supremely comfortable hotel which describes itself as a 'centre of Berber hospitality' is the base for numerous walks in the Atlas, in particular the ascent of Jbel Toubkal. Although some people attempt the mountain alone with backpacks and small rations of food and water, the preferable, more civilised option is to take a guide, a cook, a porter and a couple of load-bearing mules, all of which can be organised by the Kasbah.

We set off in a fine drizzle, sadly clad in all the waterproofs we never thought we'd need, following first a dusty road, then a riverbed and finally a narrow track that launched us on our relentless uphill route. Mohammed, our guide, doggedly led the way, all the while bravely describing a landscape we could barely decipher through the curtains of mist. We stopped for lunch, taking shelter beneath the blue tarpaulin of a hardy wayside trader (one of several on the lower

Looking one way I can see the vast emptiness of the Sahara stretching to the horizon

reaches of the mountain who cash in on the regular flow of walkers in need of a hot mint tea, chocolate, a souvenir or perhaps a new pair of earrings) where the cook conjured up hearty platefuls of couscous and meatballs. Then on, up and up to the refuge hut at 10,000 feet, the stopping place for the night.

If the summit of Jbel Toubkal was our zenith, then the refuge hut was our nadir. Most people eschew its bleak communal dormitories and putrid bathrooms in favour of camping outside. Regrettably and in spite of the fact that our trusty mule had lugged camping equipment up the mountain, it was was too cold and bleak for tents. Whether it was the smell or the altitude that did it we had no appetite for food that night, so we shut down our stomachs, closed our noses and slept the fitful sleep of those not used to 'roughing' it.

Coming up trumps

Our final ascent started before daybreak, following a more arduous route than the previous day through steep gullies of boulders, across swathes of scree and pockets of snow. Each step on that three-hour climb became harder than the last as the air thinned and a mild dizziness set in. Walking above 10,000 feet is as much about mental strength as physical agility and there's no rhyme or reason as to who altitude sickness affects, though children are often said to feel it more. Oddly enough, my boy suffered most on the way down. With the challenge of reaching the top behind him and a full day's walk back to the Kasbah

above **A room with a view ...**

right **... and what a view it was**

ahead of him, exhaustion and dehydration began to take its toll. So the good old mule came up trumps again, carrying him down the mountain to our starting point.

It's evening now and as I sit on the rooftop terrace of the Kasbah sipping mint tea and admiring the towering peaks around me I get into conversation with a Swiss-German Alpinist who we've encountered on various stages of our walk. He tells me that it's a huge achievement for a boy so young to climb a mountain so high. I must be a proud father, he adds. I am, I tell him, and so is the boy in question who, having fully recovered his strength, can now revel in his success.

opposite **Gullies and boulders on the way up**
above **Triumph at the summit**

above left **Our trusty donkey**

IDEAL AGE: 10–16

Kasbah du Toubkal, Marrakech, Morocco
Tel: + 33 466 458395
www.kasbahdutoubkal.com

Double rooms from €150
Trekking prices on request

TIP
• *The ascent of Jbel Toubkal is best undertaken between May and September*

CHINESE CRACKERS

China

'One day we will walk on the Great Wall of China,' said my wife to my daughter. It was a rash thing to promise but it was a wet Sunday afternoon in Oxford and they'd just been watching *Mulan* together. I've never understood what's quite so empowering about *Mulan* but girls like it and so when I saw this trip – Chinese Crackers: with Children – advertised in the paper I thought that finally we could live the dream. Of course, what had happened in the intervening five years is that Livvie has grown up and developed attitude and today, as we sweat and stagger up and down the damn Wall, my wife is walking with me because her daughter would rather hang out with the other proto-teens who are off ahead, bitching about their parents.

Don't get me wrong. Visiting China with children can be delightful. For a start they are treated like super-stars. Livvie quickly got used to being asked to pose, like a grinning giraffe, alongside school parties of local kids and the Great Wall is as great as it says on the box. It's broad, chunky and indomitable, snaking up and down vertiginous slopes the full length of China's mountainous border as it stood back in the third century BC. The only problem is that our party of five nuclear families is dogged by local vendors who sprint alongside us chanting, 'Coca-Cola-water-ice-beer, Coca-Cola-water-ice-beer!' – all at exorbitant prices.

We don't see Livvie till the end of the day, when we find her giving piggyback rides to the younger children. She is seemingly unaffected by our long hot march.

'Well at least she's enjoying herself,' says my wife as we clamber back into the minibus, gagging for the air conditioning to be switched on. August is not a good month to go on holiday in China, which is a shame as that's when the cheapest trips run from the UK. Still a package tour is by far the best way to see the country. Chinese bureaucracy is a nightmare and outside the big cities very few people speak English. Besides which the kids clearly enjoy the company of other children.

The next day in Tiananmen Square we found ourselves caught up in a mass-orgy of photography. In front of Mao's mausoleum there was a regular scrum of Oriental and Occidental children, all wearing Beijing 2008 baseball caps, making peace signs and giggling at each other as parents flashed away with their cameras. All this fuss made our children feel like stars – no bad start to a holiday.

Our next stop was the Forbidden City, which turned out to be much more fun than any of us expected.

All this fuss made our children feel like stars – no bad start to a holiday

Nobody had told me there was a Starbucks inside, just next to the Gate of Heavenly Purity, so there were frappucinos all round and I got my first shot of espresso in days. And the shopping opportunities! Livvie, who had eschewed an 'I Walked the Great Wall' T-shirt, went berserk, buying up little silk purses and make-up bags from as little as ten yuan (seventy pence) as Christmas presents for all her friends. We left her in the Olympics 2008 shop, just opposite the Gate of Heavenly Caffeine, because she was revelling in her purchasing power and didn't want to come and see the Imperial Garden with us. We fixed a time when we'd all meet up again at the shop.

Livvie's good sense

Unfortunately, unbeknownst to any of us, this was the same time that the president of Venezuela was due to be shown round the Forbidden City. Suddenly, as we were making our way back from the Palace of Earthly Tranquillity, we were caught in a melee of tourists being pushed out of the way by skinny teenaged soldiers whose batons were making sure the president got a clear run of the place. We explained that our daughter was waiting for us, and my wife burst into tears, but we still were not allowed through for another half an hour. The soldiers were very young and adamant and left me with a disturbing impression of what the Red Guard must have been like. Fortunately, when we were finally allowed back through we found Livvie had had the good sense to stay in the shop, although she had pretty much disposed of all her holiday pocket money. We were so relieved we loaned her some extra yuan, but I know my wife won't be voting for Mr Chavez any time soon.

Happily reunited, mother and daughter set off that evening for the Beijing Acrobats with the other members of our party. They had a good story to tell everyone and that is part of the pleasure of a group tour: there's always an immediate audience for your adventures.

I missed that particular event, suspecting (correctly) that it would be naff. Instead I took a walk to the Temple of Heaven. This downtown park has a relaxed feel to it. In the days when the Emperor had a direct line to the gods he would process here annually to persuade the deities to grant another bumper harvest. Nowadays it's no longer divine – just a much-needed green space in Beijing with some beautiful conical temples. Along the zigzag Long Corridor I found old men playing cards and mah-jong. Chinese musicians were jamming on the most bizarre collection of pipes, cymbals and drums and a middle-aged lady was dancing with her granddaughter. There was even a mixed choir having an impromptu and very enthusiastic rehearsal. While I felt privileged to wander into this scene of simple pleasures I couldn't help wishing that Livvie was with me too. She would have enjoyed the sense of happiness I saw in those people and they would certainly have enjoyed her.

It's not every child that gets an entire nation queuing up to have their photograph taken with her.

> Along the zigzag Long Corridor I found old men playing cards and mah-jong

opposite **National treasures in China**

TIPS

- *Do go with a package tour for value and for safety's sake*
- *Take plenty of toilet tissue (it's hardly ever available in the public lavatories), antibacterial hand gel and warn your children in advance about squat toilets*
- *Chinese fizzy drinks are cheap and good value, Chinese beer is perfectly fine and comes in enormous bottles. Avoid Chinese wine*
- *Stock up on bottled water and snacks at local supermarkets rather than tourist venues*
- *Make sure before you set off exploring that you have your destination or your hotel written down or on a business card in Chinese for your taxi driver*

IDEAL AGE: 11–16

For details of family-friendly holidays in China contact Holidays from Heaven
Tel + 44 (0) 118 933 3777
www.holidaysfromheaven.com

FINDING THEIR FEET

India

If you're up for it – and many people won't be – a holiday with your kids in India could give you and your family the time of your lives. India is one of the most child friendly nations on earth, its people are warm and welcoming and childcare is readily available at all likely holiday destinations. Rich in its colours, intoxicating in its smells with myriad sights and sounds India is an enchanting place for children and can turn the heads of even the most hardened western urban dwellers.

To avoid both the intense heat and the wild monsoon season, the best time to visit is between September and April, taking advantage of the October or February half-terms, and the Christmas or Easter holidays. The warm temperatures at these times of the year also make packing easy. Essentials really only include sunhat, sun cream and a basic set of summer clothes. Anyway Indian laundry services are among the best in the world and your clothes will be returned washed, fresh and ironed in a flash.

When travelling with a family it's unwise to undertake the backpacker routes, rather select a single destination which will provide enough interest of its own and provide a base from which to explore. I have chosen four destinations, which are family friendly,

comfortable and provide everything necessary for an exciting and rewarding holiday. They are set in the diverse but equally beautiful areas of India: Rajasthan in the north-east, Goa in the south-east and land-locked Madhya Pradesh in the centre of the country.

The Ahilya Fort in Madhya Pradesh is heaven for kids. The majestic 250-year-old fort, now a charming hotel, sits on the edge of a cliff, high above the sacred Narmada River. It's a huge rambling place with a lovely, secluded swimming pool, acres of garden to explore and its very own 'living' temple. The river provides entertainment for everyone with inner tube rides for children ending in a picnic at some idyllic riverside spot, and boat rides at dusk for adults with a sundowner followed by dinner under a full moon. Should you wish to venture further afield, the hotel is situated near the beautiful and unexplored town of Maheshwar and the deserted city of Mandu, one of India's rarely visited highlights.

With direct flights available from Europe and America, Goa offers perfect beach holidays for families. For most of the year temperatures are perfect and the sea is wonderfully warm and safe, even the monsoon in Goa is fabulous as everyone comes out to dance and celebrate the onset of the rains. The Taj Exotica

India is one of the most child friendly nations on earth

above and opposite **Rural Rajasthan**

The views are spectacular by day and the night skies are ablaze with stars

hotel, in the south, is situated a stone's throw from one of the state's most stunning beaches. It also boasts huge gardens, a large swimming pool and a light and airy atmosphere. When tired of relaxing on the beach, Goa has plenty to offer by way of exploration – take a cruise up the Mandovi River and sail through mangrove swamps and past riverside villages; visit the beautiful churches scattered around the state; and see the magnificent buildings of Old Goa.

Dreams of Rajasthan

For a completely different experience the family run Wilderness Camp in Rohet near Jodhpur in Rajasthan offers an exotic new take on the word 'camping'. The camp boasts six large and luxurious tents (with attached bathrooms with running hot and cold water), which sit on top of a small sand dune in the middle of the natural wilderness of the Thar Desert. The views are spectacular by day and the night skies are ablaze with stars. Apart from the odd noise from passing camels and goats, accompanied by shepherds' song, one can almost hear the silence. For children it's something never to be forgotten as they experience true desert life in its fullest and most unspoiled form. During the day you can go out riding; picnicking at a watering hole; spend a few hours wandering

around the desert on a camel; or simply sit and enjoy the peace and let your children run wild – there are no roads or threats out here. In the early mornings and late afternoons, go out in a jeep to see the abundant wildlife that thrives in the desert and visit the local communities who will welcome you into their homes, which are alive with coy, giggling children peeping around corners at you. For a more cultural experience, you can take a short ride on the train into Jodhpur to explore the mighty fort which broods silently over the city, or you can drive over to Rohet Garh for a swim in the pool and to explore the surrounding village. There is so much to do that a week will pass in a flash. Time here offers a rare glimpse into the heart of rural Rajasthan – the Golden Triangle can wait for gap-year travellers.

If Rajasthan appeals to you but camping doesn't then the sumptuous Samode Palace or the Deogarh Mahal, a dream-like fort-palace hotel, which sits on a small hilltop in the middle of one of the state's loveliest villages, might be just the thing. Run by the whole family, it's a rambling building with endless different wings to explore and is ideal for children as the family have children of their own who love making friends with the guests. With table tennis, snooker, enclosed swimming pool, elephants' stables and old

opposite (clockwise from top) **Narmada River sunset, the Samode Palace, inside and out**

above **Camping Rohet-style**   below **Ahilya Fort view**

royal bedrooms, no child will ever get bored. The village itself offers all sorts of fascinating trinkets in an endless, vibrant maze of streets. The surrounding scenery is stunning as it sits in the Aravalli Hills, a short drive brings you to the majestic Kumbhalgarh fort and the incredible Jain temples of Ranakpur. For venturing out beyond the village, a ride on the local train is beautiful, through tunnels, hills, woodland and villages. And for an active alternative you can go for long walks or rides and have picnics at deserted forts overlooking miles and miles of extraordinary rolling hills.

The India that children will most enjoy encompasses running free, local wildlife and the people rather than ogling gem-encrusted mogul temples. Adults too will enjoy the pastoral way of life and the pleasure of seeing their children find their feet in one of the most colourful countries on earth.

IDEAL AGE: 8–16

For tailor-made tours and holidays in India contact Holidays from Heaven
Tel + 44 (0) 118 933 3777
www.holidaysfromheaven.com

Safari

Going on safari sees the great outdoors at its most exciting. Raw, natural encounters with the wild serve as Mother Nature's aphrodisiac. We fall in love with our planet over and over again as we watch each new sighting bring a fresh revelation. Like thousands of others, I'm in awe of the African bush and its unique offerings. Experiencing the circle of life unfold its magic is something all children should encounter at least once. It's a holiday of a lifetime and one they'll never forget.

KNOCK KNOCK, WHO'S THERE?

Giraffe Manor, Kenya

In less than a century, Nairobi has grown from a swampy watering hole used by Masai tribesmen into the largest city between Cairo and Johannesburg. Thousands of travellers pass through Kenya's capital each year en route to an east African safari, but very few linger long enough to explore its lively, cosmopolitan streets.

This is a shame because modern Nairobi offers more than enough entertainment for visitors. Nor need you be in a hurry to fly out again to distant safari destinations: just outside the city, Nairobi National Park's 117 square kilometres of plains, cliffs and forest are home to herds of zebra, wildebeest and buffalo as large as anywhere in Kenya. Not to mention the rhinos, cheetahs and lions – all to be found within twenty minutes of the central business district. Then there is Daphne Sheldrick's famous elephant orphanage, where you can visit (and sponsor) baby elephants being nursed back to health before release into the wild. The excellent museum is worth a visit, as is the home of Karen Blixen, author of *Out of Africa*.

Of the dozens of places to stay in and around the Nairobi National Park, the most unusual must surely be Giraffe Manor, tucked away in the leafy suburb of Karen on the edge of the park. Built in 1932, this elegant mansion, surrounded by 140 acres of its own park and forest, provides an oasis of calm in the bustling city, and is an idyllic spot to spend a night or two.

On first impression, you could be forgiven for thinking you were in an aristocratic English mansion rather than an African home – but a glance out of the window at the giraffes strolling gracefully outside instantly dispels that misapprehension. The two original Rothschild giraffes brought to the manor by Jock Leslie-Melville in the 1970s have, by now, multiplied into a thriving herd, whose delightfully bold members are never very far away.

Breakfast on the first floor

Our first encounter with the giraffes came almost as soon as we arrived, when one of the younger ones appeared through a downstairs window. It knew the routine well, and my children were soon giggling with delight as they held out pony nuts to be scooped up by a surprisingly blue and very long tongue. The excitement continued the following morning when a visitor appeared at our first-floor bedroom window, guzzling down two buckets of nuts in no time at all. Giraffes really are delightful animals, and it is a rare treat to get so close to them.

My children were soon giggling with delight as they held out pony nuts to be scooped up by a surprisingly blue and very long tongue

The house was opened to visitors when Leslie-Melville died, and is now a thriving small hotel. The six rooms are comfortable rather than luxurious, but the antiques and treasures gathered over the years, together with the family photographs hanging on many of the walls, help to create a homely atmosphere. The drawing room, in particular, is crammed full of interesting books, and is the perfect place to wile away an hour or two.

The hotel also lives up to its claim to have 'one of the finest kitchens in Nairobi'. Guests sit together in the elegant dining room, exchanging safari stories. Lunch is fairly relaxed, with delicious soups and pasta the order of the day, while dinner, preceded by drinks in the drawing room, is a more formal, candle-lit occasion. Children are well catered for, with early mealtimes or specially prepared food available on request.

The staff at the manor can arrange a number of activities. There are some lovely walks through the park, which is home to 180 bird species, as well as warthogs and bushbucks. Just across the garden from the manor is the Giraffe Centre, which is open to the public as well as hotel guests. This excellent facility, originally opened for use by local schoolchildren, tells you just about everything you could possibly want know about giraffes, as well as a host of other wildlife, and is worth a visit. The guides are extremely informative, and there are plenty more opportunities to feed the long-necked residents. The income generated by the entrance fees to the Centre supports other conservation projects all over Kenya.

above **Feeding time for the local residents**

above **The nearby Giraffe Centre provides copious amounts of information about these spectacular animals**

Guests sit
together in the
elegant dining
room, exchanging
safari stories

IDEAL AGE: 3–16

Giraffe Manor, PO Box 15004, Langata 00509, Kenya
Tel + 254 (0) 20 891 078
www.giraffemanor.com

6 rooms
Daily inclusive charge per person US$327.50 full board

The Master room interconnects with the Giraffe room,
which has two beds suitable for family members,
chargeable at half the standard rate

BORN FREE
Rekero Camp, Kenya

Kenya's Masai Mara is perhaps the most famous of all Africa's game parks. Its 1,812 square kilometres contain some stunning scenery and a truly awe-inspiring amount of game, including the annual migration of hundreds of thousands of wildebeest across the plains, in search of fresh grazing. The river crossings en route offer spectacular – if gory – viewing of that remarkable phenomenon, as the shaggy, ungainly creatures attempt to dodge the enormous crocodiles lying in wait for them.

To concentrate merely on the migration, though, would be to miss out on the many other splendours of the Mara, such as its huge number of big cats, its fantastic variety of plain game, and its elephants and few elusive rhinos. It also boasts a rich cultural history, and the Masai tribes people still live their traditional life on the outskirts of the reserve.

Ron Beaton, one of the names in Kenya's safari history, founded Rekero in 1987. Having lived in this wild and beautiful corner of the park for many years, Ron and his family have extensive knowledge of the animals and their habits, and they delight in passing on their passion and knowledge to all who stay with them. Ron has now handed over the day-to-day running of this delightful camp to his eldest son,

Gerard, and co-owner and local Masai Jackson Looseyia, both of whom infuse the camp with their youthful energy and sense of fun.

Rekero is a forty-five-minute light aircraft flight followed by a short game drive from Nairobi. Guests' first view on arriving at the mess area (safari for reception) is of the Talek River, gently meandering past the seven tents set just above the riverbank. Looking across the river at the plain beyond, you are treated to an ever-changing view of Africa; one minute elegant giraffes pick at tall trees, the next a troop of noisy baboons scramble down to the river, then some zebra wander past, serenading you with their distinctive grunting neigh.

Families are welcome at Rekero, as long as parents and children realise that the camp is not fenced – and may well be visited by lions or buffalo during the night. We were greeted by Jackson, whose traditional Masai *shuka* (red cloak) and accompanying spear immediately gave him the boys' undivided attention. He assured us they would be fine sharing their own tent, and then set about showing them how everything worked. They mastered the African plumbing and myriad tent zips in no time, and were delighted to feel like grown-ups involved in a real adventure.

Guests' first view on arriving is of the Talek River, gently meandering past the seven tents set just above the riverbank

The seven tents are well spread out along the river – each around ten metres from the next. Inside they are comfortably furnished with proper beds, simple wardrobes and an en-suite toilet. They also have a bucket shower: a wonderful contraption rather like a giant watering can, which is filled and then hoisted into a tree for the ultimate outdoor showering experience. There is cold running water and staff will provide hot water whenever required. Each tent has its own private verandah overlooking the river; there is no electricity, but the solar lights are sufficient for bedtime reading.

Best game viewing in the world

The majority of game viewing here is vehicle-based, and the experience of the local Masai and Ndorobo guides is such that guests from Rekero are unlikely to encounter other tourists during their stay. After a pre-dawn wake-up call, game drives set off just as the sun is rising. Family groups are – as far as possible – allocated their own vehicle and guide so that parents don't have to deal with the nightmare of their children disrupting other guests' viewing. This also means the drives can be adapted so they are interesting to the children as well as the adults. Our two sons – displaying that innate fascination with weaponry that most boys have – had been furnished with Masai bows and arrows early on during our stay, and our guide, James, was perfectly happy to assist with target practice when we stopped for a bush breakfast each morning.

Food on safari is rarely a disappointment and Rekero is no exception. The breakfasts are produced effortlessly after a couple of hours' viewing. The guides pick a picturesque spot – perhaps on the riverbank or on a hilltop with a spectacular view – and then proceed to unpack cereal, homemade bread, muffins, coffee and fruit juice. There are also Scotch eggs: a little strange at breakfast, but actually quite welcome: it is surprising how hungry you get after the very early start.

On returning to camp, there is enough time for a quick shower and change before lunch, when more wonderful homemade fare is served. Taken outside under a couple of shady trees, the meal is interrupted every so often by animal happenings on the river below. And just in case you are still hungry, high tea is served before the evening game drive.

After sundown, guests return to camp to discuss the day's sightings over drinks around the fire. Children

above **Jackson Looseyia with new recruit and old friend**

above **Lunch safari-style**   above right **Tented luxury**

The guides
go out of their
way to entertain
the children
with increasingly
wild stories

are made particularly welcome, and the guides go out of their way to entertain them with increasingly wild stories. This is followed by a three-course dinner taken either under the stars or, if rain threatens, in the cosy mess tent. After dinner, sleepy children can be accompanied to their tents by an *Askari* (a spear-holding Masai nightwatchman), who will wait on the verandah until their parents return. This is one of the few occasions when an early bedtime is not met with the usual feet-dragging reluctance.

Since it is prepared in a bush kitchen, dinner is necessarily simple. You don't get fancy haute cuisine, but what you do get is delicious, fresh, home-cooked food, with enough variety to satisfy everyone. And with a bit of warning, the camp chef is well able to cater for various dietary requirements.

Rekero is one of those rare gems whose staff and hosts have the knack of making everyone, from youngsters to grandparents, feel extremely welcome. The Masai Mara offers some of the best game viewing in the world, and the thrill of seeing it bought to life by fantastic guides is second to none.

You don't get fancy haute cuisine, but what you do get is delicious, home-cooked food

IDEAL AGE: 8–16

Rekero Lodge, Masai Mara, PO Box 56923, Nairobi 00200, Kenya
www.rekero.com
Contact the lodge directly at
rekerocamp@africaonline.co.ke

7 tents
Daily inclusive charge from US$425 per person plus camp fees

ONE BIG GAME

Ant's Nest, South Africa

South Africa is often referred to as a 'world in one country', and it is easy to see why. The options for visitors are manifold: cosmopolitan Cape Town, the gorgeous Cape coast, the chic safari lodges of the Kruger National Park and the stunning scenery of the Drakensberg mountains are just some of them.

Tucked away in the Limpopo Province, around three hours' drive north-west of Johannesburg, lies the Waterberg region. This sparsely populated area is typified by low mountain ranges and escarpments, interlaced with rivers, streams and swamps. It is also home to around seventy-five mammal species, including big game such as elephant, lion, hippo, leopard, buffalo and white and black rhino.

It is here, on a huge private game reserve, that Ant and Tessa Baber run Ant's Nest, and if ever there was a paradise for children, then this must be it. The lodge itself has been built around the original homestead and still retains the homely atmosphere of a working farm. Guests are greeted with cool drinks on the shady verandah at the front of the main building from which you can see the gardens, surrounded by pretty flower-beds and shrubs. The pool at the end of the garden, with its shady thatched area, is also visible, as are the horses, grazing contentedly in the bush just beyond.

The Babers run Ant's Nest as their home, and guests are entertained as part of the family. On the whole, the lodge is booked on an exclusive basis so that family groups have the place to themselves and can decide exactly what they want to do and when they want to do it. The Babers' aim is 'to provide a uniquely flexible safari experience, offering guests a wide choice of activities, keeping everyone entertained from the youngest to the oldest, the fittest to the most in need of a rest.' Having stayed there twice myself, I would say they accomplish all that with ease.

Wonderful African fabrics and furniture

Each of the six en-suite bedrooms is luxuriously appointed. Tessa, who was brought up in Kenya, has put to good use her wonderful eye for African fabrics and furniture. Hand-carved beds swathed in gently flowing fabrics, tables decorated with porcupine quills and ostrich eggs, and huge open-air balconies all elicit a feeling of peace and relaxation. The communal areas are also furnished invitingly, with comfy sofas and tables: perfect for sundowners or after-dinner drinks.

The reserve itself encompasses a diverse range of habitats, from open plains to mountainous regions,

Hand-carved beds swathed in gently flowing fabrics, tables decorated with porcupine quills and ostrich eggs

above **Bird's-eye view**

and sustains a wide variety of game, including the rare sable antelope, nyala, oryx, eland, giraffe, buffalo, white rhino and well over 300 bird species. Days tend to start early, with guests setting off after a quick breakfast on either a ride or a game drive into the reserve. Ant, who acts as chief guide, has an encyclopedic knowledge of the bush and is a wonderfully entertaining companion whether you are game-viewing from a vehicle (perhaps with a bit of gentle walking thrown in), on foot, or on horseback.

Even inexperienced riders can enjoy the horseback rides and, since there are no big cats to worry about, you are unlikely to need to gallop out of trouble. Riding is a wonderful way to explore the bush since a horse's presence makes the animals less skittish than a vehicle. Riding with my children among zebra and giraffes is something that will stay with me for a long time.

During the heat of the day, parents can relax by the pool while the children raid the toy box, containing everything from cricket and football equipment to card and board games. The flat garden also provides a safe play area – so long as parents keep an eye out for the occasional resident rhino nibbling at the flowerbeds.

Exploration begins again in the late afternoon, whether your family's preference is for checking on the sable herd, tracking a pregnant rhino or any number of other activities. Children's interest in the running of the reserve can also be indulged; road clearing armed with *pangas* (small axes) was a particular favourite on one of our visits. If, on the other hand, your children have had enough or simply want a rest then childcare can be arranged at the lodge while you continue sightseeing.

above and opposite **Up close and personal**

Food is taken very seriously at Ant's Nest, and the chef's sumptuous home-cooked meals are eaten outside whenever possible. There's nothing better after a couple of hours' riding or walking to find a bush breakfast all laid out for you on your return. At night, supper is taken around open fires under the stars, and, if it is late, no one minds children appearing in pyjamas. Early mealtimes are also available if your family prefers it that way.

Anything from a three- to seven-night stay offers a perfect family introduction to the African bush. Tessa, Ant and their team are marvellous hosts, the area is malaria-free and there is such a wide variety of activities on offer that it is almost impossible to get bored.

IDEAL AGE: 6–16

Ant's Nest, PO Box 441, Vaalwater, 0530, South Africa
Tel + 27 14 755 3584
www.waterberg.net

6 rooms
Prices on request

Special food and meal times can be arranged and children are welcome to come to
supper in their dressing gowns
Full childminding facilities are also available

OVERLAND ADVENTURE

Kenya to Zanzibar

If you missed out on the gap-year experience and are now tied to a nine-to-five routine, with two point four kids (who want to come too) then a family overland tour might just be the answer to your prayers. But if the thought of Africa's grit under your fingernails or its dust on your teeth makes you shudder, stop reading now.

Overlanding, as it's popularly called, can be described in many ways: a journey, a life experience, even an endurance feat, but one thing it is not is a picnic in the park. Instead, it offers camaraderie, safe adventure and a passage across some of Africa's most iconic scenery.

Really wild show

And so it was that we found ourselves in Nairobi on day one of a daunting fifteen-night expedition, with all the gear and no idea what to expect. Yes, the brochure described the route and the detailed trip notes had prepared us on 'what to do and what not to do'. But – and it was a big but – what would the trip leaders and other passengers be like?

In the event, we felt lucky. Our ten fellow adult travellers, from Australia, Canada and England, seemed a cheery bunch, while the twelve children, who ranged from seven to thirteen-years-old, seemed to bond immediately. Vicky, the trip leader, Jason, the assistant, and Charles, the Kenyan cook, instantaneously allayed all our fears with their calm, authoritative but friendly manner; we were confident they knew exactly what they were doing.

A mellow orientation around Nairobi included visits to Giraffe Manor and the David Sheldrick Wildlife Trust, home to eight orphaned elephants. Like humans, elephants need company, love and a place to explore (boredom turns them psychotic). Ten-month-old McKenna backed into the crowd, close enough for the children to feel the coarseness of his prickly spinal hairs and soft inquisitive nostrils.

From Nairobi it was a three-hour drive to our first stop. The stunning Great Rift Valley never fails to provoke a gasp – the largest split in the earth's crust runs straight through Kenya, characterised by both fresh and volcanic lakes and filled with exotic wildlife, including hippos and flamingos. We stopped at a spot where the sheer cliffs fell over 1,000 metres into the valley. On the eastern rift, we could see the first of the seven lakes that run the length of Kenya's rift: Lake Naivasha, home to Joy Adamson of *Born Free* fame.

Boats took us through the papyrus grasses to the

The stunning Great Rift Valley never fails to provoke a gasp – the largest split in the earth's crust runs straight through Kenya

above **Flamingos on Lake Nakuru**   below **Lions in the Serengeti**

jetty of Joy's lakeside home (now a museum), where long-haired colobus monkeys clambered through branches beside electric-blue starlings and lilac-breasted rollers. The ride along the bumpy unmade road from Naivasha to Gilgil (barely forty kilometres) took nearly three hours.

We had come to visit the twenty-seven children of the House of Hope Orphanage, founded by retired nurse, Jill Simpson, who could not ignore the urgent need for children's shelter. Jill's aim to provide 'love, safety, comfort, support, food and shelter' and to 'help the children face tomorrow' is actively supported by Dragoman, the company we were travelling with.

After a five o'clock start the following morning we arrived at Lake Nakuru, where thousands of flamingos covered the white soda lake in currents of

above **Electric blue starling**
below **Colobus monkey at Niavasha**

Thousands
of flamingos
covered the
white soda lake
in currents of
pink chiffon

pink chiffon. Created as a bird sanctuary in 1961, it now protects rhino, leopards and hyena as well. After a night surrounded by noisy wildlife, we stopped on the western escarpment, known as Baboon Cliffs, for a fry-up with a panoramic view.

Keep on trucking

By day three everyone had settled into their tour duties: locker loading, kitty tallying, water collection for scrupulous hand washing, campfire duty and truck cleaning. Life consisted of pre-dawn starts, continual erecting and taking down of tents and long days on the road followed by cooking or truck duties. There was little time for personal relaxation or exploration – which was a test for all.

At Njoro we upgraded to a farmstead cottage (with

loos and hot water – now a luxury) before the long drive through the highland tea and sugarcane plantations to the eastern shores of Lake Victoria across the border in Tanzania. The glacially moulded landscape and adobe settlements lent an ancient feel that felt a world away from Kenya.

The truck was loaded up with stores for the next three days, which were spent driving through the Serengeti Plains (Masai for 'the place where land runs on forever'). The truck's roof became a viewing podium par excellence – with topi, Thompson's gazelle, zebra and wildebeest spotted by the dozen. But we arrived late at our camping spot and, while England was having its hottest weather since 1936, we erected tents in the dark during the mother of all thunderstorms.

All a big game

Back on the roof of the truck the following morning, our giraffe's-eye view afforded some great sights: herds of elephant, two leopards in a sausage tree and a pride of seven lions. We left the park at Naabi Hill Gate on a high and pitched our tents overlooking Ngorongoro to enjoy the view and marshmallows toasted on a campfire.

My guidebook wasn't joking when it described the road out of the Serengeti as diabolical – toe-tinglingly shaky, we lost count of the times we were buckarooed from our seats yelling 'yee-ha' all the way. The scenery became mesmerisingly inhospitable with only an occasional ostrich, wild dog or red-robed Masai herdsman steering his goats towards the clusters of sheltered mud huts.

The temperature soared as we dropped into the world's largest volcanic caldera. Ngorongoro – onomatopoeically named by the Masai after the clatter of cowbells – is dramatic, remote, arid and vast.

Perhaps the most bizarre sight was the lions slumped under the body of stationary jeeps, resting innocuously in the shade: it was hard to believe they're killers of the first degree.

this page **The House of Hope Orphanage**
opposite **The marketplace at Musoma**

above **Local Arusha Masai**

We passed Manyara National Park, Kilimanjaro and Arusha, where the market was heaving with Masai trading their cattle. Their distinctive tribal clothes were like a wash of African tartan. While the children stroked a baby hyena and marvelled at the pythons in the Meserani Snake Park, we visited the museum and were educated about Masai domestic life.

After a fourteen-hour transfer to Dar es Salaam, the pace slowed to a halt at the laid-back Kipepeo Beach – a popular backpacking haunt with a picture-perfect beach that was home to cows as well as exhausted tourists. Ten days on the road had taken its toil and we all revelled in the thought of chilling out by the sea. Finally we were on the road to Zanzibar – meaning 'the land of black people' – made rich from ivory, spice and the slave trade. Stone Town is like Marrakech-on-sea, full of young boys in pristine *dishdashers*, men with monkeys on leashes and all the hubbub of colourful market traders touting their goods. European and Omani settlers have left their mark with a fascinating fusion of Swahili and colonial buildings lining the streets – often scruffy, vacant and in need of restoration.

And there our adventure ended. The children hugged each other goodbye, exchanged promises to stay in touch and then headed with their parents to the airport. Once back at home, I blissed out in a steaming hot bubble bath and my thoughts returned to Africa

above **Eastern Zanzibar**

and to our cook, Charles, who told us he had been saving for two years to buy a $1,000 water tank for his house – the first in a community of 50,000 people.

He had mentioned it hundred times during our trip, but the full force of it didn't hit me until that moment. Most of the time, I reflected, we westerners really just don't know we're born.

IDEAL AGE: 7–16

TIP

- *You are strongly recommended to take a head torch, baby wipes and antiseptic hand cleaning gel*

Dragoman Overland, Camp Green, Debenham, Stowmarket, Suffolk IP14 6LA, UK
Tel + 44 (0) 1728 861133
www.dragoman.com

From £755 per person plus kitty from approximately US$730 per person for a fifteen-day family-based tour (excluding flights)
Age limit from seven years old

EASY ZAMBESI

Kasaka River Lodge, Zambia

Our adventure began as soon as we boarded the smart twelve-seater bush plane at Lusaka. The giant crop rotation circles, dusty terracotta scrubland and the motorway of pylons stretching to the horizon instantly made us feel a lot further than nine hours' flying time (and just one time zone) away from London.

The scenery unexpectedly morphed as we dipped to follow the course of the Lower Zambezi River along whose escarpment we could easily make out hundreds of hippos, elephants, crocodiles, buffalos, warthogs and antelopes roaming freely. The excitement was irrepressible: it was as if the children had suddenly been teleported into the raw, living Africa of their imagination.

Fenceless and defenceless

We touched down thirty minutes later on the loamy airstrip of the Kasaka River Lodge, where we were greeted by a troop of squabbling baboons. Their squeals alerted us to the fact that we were totally surrounded by wildlife – unfenced and ostensibly defenceless (a baboon is six times stronger than a man, I was reliably informed). The alien sounds and smells in the dry, dusty air pricked our senses with anticipation. I felt like a lioness watching her audacious cubs

scatter, always alert and ready to rein in their foolhardy activities.

But it is this unforgettable location that marks Kasaka out from the hordes of other luxury lodgings that fill safari brochures these days. Nestled on the bank at the confluence of the Chongwe and Zambezi Rivers, 200 kilometres downstream from Victoria Falls, the rich flood plains of the Lower Zambezi National Park support vast densities of wildlife. Add to that the surprisingly mild, non-tropical climate bestowed by landlocked Zambia's high altitude and the result is pure bliss – even if you have three children aged eleven, nine and six in tow.

The twenty-two-bed lodge, one of the few safari lodges in Zambia to accommodate children, is a dream come true for its owners, all of whom are couples and several of whom have their own young families. It consists of seven permanent tented structures (with en-suite bathrooms) and a luxurious two-bedroom 'Hippo-pod', complete with thatched roof and sturdy adobe walls: perfect for the slightly squeamish or families requiring that little extra protection.

It took some effort but my elder two persuaded me to let them sleep in their own tent under strict instruction not to put so much as a toe outside the canvas

My girls loved playing with their African counterparts, who laughed and joked as they braided their unfamiliar blonde hair

until their mugs of hot chocolate arrived in the morning. Possibly, though, that restriction was more easily agreed to than observed – what with the vervet monkeys clambering across the awnings, constant hippo grunts, and strange noises in the bushes.

A guided 'poo walk' – for children only – gave me two hours of peace and quiet the next morning: time to stare at the ancient baobab tree and watch the bee-eaters, kingfishers, egrets and fish eagles going about their daily life. The children returned buzzing with enthusiasm about the baboons and monkey-fruits they had tracked down, bursting with tales of the myriad tracks they had confidently recognised. 'We know lion, hyena, serval, genet, shrew, civet and elephant tracks,' they gushed. 'And we found hippo poo up a tree.'

Living and learning

The biggest hit was probably the tiger-fish trip: three happy girls equipped with rods and hope. As we waited for a bite, we watched elephants splashing in the river, filling their trunks and showering their shorter-nosed youngsters. A goliath heron stretched out its plumes to dry in the sun as a majestic saddle-billed stork put on a display of bill clapping, impressing both us and his prospective mate. Our patience soon paid off as a respectably sized bream was hooked, admired and released; budding conservationists wouldn't dream of eating fish for supper.

Kasaka's closest neighbour downstream is the non-profit organisation CLZ (Conservation Lower Zambezi), which protects the wildlife and habitat across 6,400 square kilometres. Particular emphasis has been placed on anti-poaching – especially of elephants, which are still being slaughtered for their tusks.

With this in mind, Adrian, the project warden, is passionately committed to educating local children (many of whom have not been fortunate enough to appreciate the beauty of their national heritage) about

above **Hippo-pod accommodation**

the effects of poaching – as well as of water pollution, fire and de-forestation. His key messages are communicated in poster-size illustrations, displayed alongside more light-hearted artefacts including a pair of bush scales which compares visitors' weights to those of various safari animals (the children weighed the same as a porcupine, an impala and a warthog respectively). The message is simple: fall in love with nature and you'll automatically endeavour to protect its legacy.

The children were also particularly entertained by a trip to the local Mugurameno School, which is strongly supported by the founders of Kasaka, a little further upstream. Attended by some 500 pupils aged between three and seventeen, it has only seven teachers, three classrooms, and no electricity or running water: just a nearby hand pump, where we watched women fill five-gallon containers and lift them onto their heads with remarkable agility.

Such is their eagerness to learn that most of the children travel many miles by foot to reach the school each day. My six-year-old entered a classroom where children were learning their times tables with the aid of sticks and beans. Within minutes she was participating as enthusiastically as the children around her. The facilities were humbling but the united spirit of the children was a joy; my girls loved playing with their African counterparts, who laughed and joked as they braided their unfamiliar blonde hair.

It was another connection they made with the beautiful country of Zambia, over and above all their memories of exotic animals and birds: a human link – and one they'll never forget.

above **Learning local skills**
opposite (clockwise from top left) **Mugurameno schoolchildren, catch of the day, visiting the classroom, a baobab tree**

TIP
- *Go between September and November for the best weather and game viewing*

IDEAL AGE : 6-16

Kasaka River Lodge, Lower Zambesi, Zambia
For bookings contact:
Simon Cooke, 69 Lowther Road, London SW13 9NP, UK
Tel +44 (0) 20 8412 0060
www.kasakariverlodge.com

7 tents from US$395 per person per night
Hippo Pod: from US$1,500 per night
Children under six on request
Prices are inclusive of all meals and park fees, walking safaris, game safaris, fishing and bush kids programme

Snow

Winter brings with it a white wonderland of fresh powdery snow, transforming mountains into an outdoor playground. Reindeers and huskies, sleighs and sleds, skis, snowboards, snowmen and a whole landscape of discovery prove an irresistible temptation to those willing to venture to colder climes. It's a giant adventure playing field for parents and children alike and one holiday that improves your health and energy levels. For children it offers an endless merry-go-round of being pulled uphill to slide back down – what could be more fun than that?

SKI-IN, SKI-OUT

Montreal and Mont Tremblant, Canada

Tremblant's instant appeal to European travellers is that it is located on Canada's accessible east coast. If landing in Montreal, a city full of attractions and family activities too tempting to miss, you could enjoy a couple of days sightseeing and dissolve the five-hour time difference.

The 350-year-old city is located on an island in the Saint Lawrence River, and offers warm hospitality with a distinctive French flavour. The must-sees include Maisonneuve Park – a wonderland for all ages. Alongside the 1976 Olympic Tower (with its funicular-type elevator and viewing platform), a huge biodome holds four of the most beautiful eco-systems of the Americas; several thousand insects are housed in the adjoining insectarium; and for two months a year 'Butterflies Go Free' in the botanical garden dome, landing on jumpers, heads and unsuspecting noses.

Unlike most North American cities, Montreal has succeeded in conserving its historic city centre which has a distinctive European flavour and is full of picturesque squares and cobblestoned streets fronting the old port. Visitors often choose a *calèche* (horse-drawn carriage) to tour the old quarter, culminating in the not-to-be-missed Notre-Dame Basilica.

Downtown, the Fairmont Queen Elizabeth hotel, of Yoko Ono and John Lennon Bed-In fame, is ideally located for easy access to shopping and sightseeing. The new 'white glove' service at the recently renovated hotel makes planning your trip so much easier: The concierge will contact you in the UK before departure to ascertain the type of activities you favour, and arrange anything from car hire to museum passes to ensure your precious holiday time is kept hassle-free.

Up into the mountains

From Montreal, the charming pedestrianised village of Tremblant, with its cheery multi-coloured rooftops, is a mere eighty-minute drive. Situated between a ribbon of lakes in the heart of the Laurentian Mountains, often cited as the world's oldest peaks, Tremblant is in fact a relatively new resort developed in the 1990s, and is currently eastern America's largest skiing area with ninety-four runs spread over 600 acres.

Opposite the frozen waters of Lac Tremblant, the impressive Fairmont hotel enjoys its ski-in ski-out location at the foot of the nursery slopes and is only a minute's walk to the hub of activity in the main square. Its cosy Québécois ambience, open log fires,

Situated between a ribbon of lakes in the heart of the Laurentian Mountains, often cited as the world's oldest peaks

antler-adorned walls, indigenous portraits and maple-leaf patterned carpets are all unmistakably Canadian. At the end of an exhilarating day, guests flock back to soothe their limbs in the indoor or outdoor pools or lie in the open-air hot tubs and Jacuzzi before a bit of pampering at the Amerispa – try a Vichy shower massage or sensuous maple-sugar body scrub.

Each day starts with a huge buffet breakfast in the Windigo restaurant. Waffles and lashings of maple syrup are de rigueur and the perfect fuel for a full day's skiing. Après ski, the extensive choice of regional gourmet cuisine includes delights such as east coast lobster with eggplant 'caviar' and marinated Alberta beef with sundried tomatoes.

Expansive two-bedroom suites, overlooking the lake or village, are perfect for families, and some have well-equipped kitchenettes ideal for preparing easy informal suppers of delicacies bought from the plethora of local delis. Alternatively, choose one of the contemporary seventh-floor Fairmont Gold rooms that offer a few extra facilities including all day refreshments and private check-in.

Fast workers

Skiing and boarding are the main activities for most guests visiting Tremblant, where snow is guaranteed with the aid of a massive artificial snowmaking system of over 800 snow cannons. Both children and adults are in for a treat when it comes to lessons. Whether you're a beginner or an expert, you'll marvel at the improvements you can achieve in just a couple of hours.

Instructors assemble children into sensibly sized groups of no more than three (for children aged three and four) and seven (for ages five to twelve). A four-day ski-week lasts from nine o'clock until three o'clock each day and is taught by enthusiastic expert teachers who really know how to motivate youngsters – and, of course, there's no language barrier.

If you're not a skiing or boarding fanatic, Tremblant has more activities than you can wave a ski at. Dog sledding, mountain sleigh rides, snowshoeing, snowmobiling and skating (all early- to mid-season),

left **Follow the leader**

opposite **Snowy mountain fun**
above **Stunning mountain scenery**

as well as tubing, riding, ice climbing and, for rainy days, ceramic painting for all the family at the art studio. For the sweet-toothed, a meal in a local *cabane à sucre* – a traditional log cabin where maple syrup is made (unique to this part of the world) – offers an entire meal cooked in the sweet sap with maple beer to wash it down.

Whatever you choose to do in Tremblant, skiing in Canada's great outdoors is an experience not to be missed, and the children will beg to return year after year.

IDEAL AGE: 3–16

Fairmont Tremblant, 3045 Chemin de la Chapelle, Mont Tremblant, Quebec, Canada J8E 1E1
Tel + 1 (819) 681 7000
www.fairmont.com/tremblant

316 rooms
Double rooms from US$227

Various Ski Clubs and Kidz Clubs are available at this resort

WE ARE THE CHAMPIONS

Zermatt, Switzerland

The combination of the iconic Matterhorn, flawlessly groomed pistes, enchanting Alpine architecture and vibrant resort life has meant that Zermatt is rarely out-ranked as one of the world's top five ski resorts. Its ski area actually covers three different mountain zones including a link over to the Italian resort of Cervinia. And as one of the highest and largest terrains in Europe you can ski a massive 2,200 vertical metres from the top of the Klein Matterhorn (3,800 metres) all the way back to the village.

Horse-drawn sleighs and small electric taxis replace cars along the narrow roads and the high street is choc-a-bloc with hotels and restaurants, boutiques and rickety wooden *mazots* that are still used for sheltering livestock and storing grain through the winter. I'd wanted to go there ever since I was a little girl when my head had been filled with stories my great aunt told, of hiking up the Matterhorn to the sound of cow bells, in search of eidleweis and spring gentians. From then on every image of that pyramidal mountain nagged at me to pay this beautiful corner of Switzerland a visit.

We'd skied in Canada with English-speaking teachers and in France with French-speaking teachers and knew, only too well, which option the children preferred.

So how could we ski in Switzerland with graspable lessons? The answer came in a bright coloured brochure – Powder Byrne 'Skiing without Compromise'. It offered the perfect trio – skiing in Europe's best scenery with top-notch coaching and accommodation.

Comfortable but not too smart

We could choose from a number of hotels (no gap-year run chalets here) including the rather swanky Mont Cervin, which looked deliciously extravagant but not right for energetic kids, who wouldn't thank me for a week of strict table manners and keeping quiet. Instead we settled on its sister hotel, the Schweizerhof; central, comfortable but not too smart, conveniently located in the centre of town close to the Gornergrat railway and five minutes from the Sunnegga Express ski lift and lots of child-friendly dining options including the folkloric Schwyzerstübli, fine Italian Da Mario and Alpine Prato Borni.

It was also home to Powder Byrne's crèche (not that we needed it) and quite the meeting place for a bit of après ski exercise. Families still energetic after skiing made use of the swimming pool, steam bath, sauna and massage rooms in the basement. We opted for one of the interconnecting bedrooms at the rear

Horse-drawn sleighs and small electric taxis replace cars along the narrow roads

above and opposite **Putting them through their paces**

of the hotel – although the street was normally quiet after eleven o'clock.

The first clue of what 'without compromise' meant was when the charming Ed came to orientate us around the resort and even carried the kids' skis back to the locker room. He explained exactly how the clubs worked, 'After the crèche we've got the Yeti Club – divided into Primer, Junior and Plus groups – for three- to nine-year-olds', he said. 'Then SnoZone for ten- to fourteen-year-olds able to manage red runs and ski all day without getting too tired. And for top level skiers confident on black runs we've got three clubs: Ultimate Zone, which teaches rescue and survival techniques; Mountain Zone for powder and off-piste techniques; and Freestyle Clinic for learning park 'n' pipe tricks from a European champion.' My two Yetis and a SnoZoner couldn't wait to hit the slopes.

Speaking of champions, Powder Byrne hit a winning idea when they decided to avail themselves of Olympian, Martin Bell, to run a ski-camp for 'trainees' as he calls them, aged between eleven and fifteen. My wannabe champion was immediately up for the challenge of rigorous days on-piste, rounded up with evening talks and video analysis to help improve her style. After five days his four trainees had one word firmly lodged in their grey matter, 'Angulation'. Endless comical exercises developing hip and shoulder angles accompanied with apparently technical terms about doing 'moonies' uphill and flashing your chest downhill, were not in vain. Martin's saintly patience combined with the rare ability to give corrective commentary that could actually be understood resulted in some pretty slick skiing not to mention, impressed parents.

Eating to your heart's content
With offspring gainfully occupied, parents can choose how to spend their days. Most plump for the complimentary guided skiing with fellow parents of similar skiing standards, meeting up for lunch in one of the chocolate-boxy timbered chalets on which Zermatt has made its name.

Zermatt's mountain restaurants are unparalled scenically and, while they're not cheap, the variety

Powder Byrne hit a winning idea when they decided to avail themselves of Olympian, Martin Bell

and quality of the food and sheer ambiance make every lunch a treat in itself. Years of belt-loosening research, our guide enthused, had resulted in a few favourites, and he was happy to share them with us. On the Sunnegga side we enjoyed the view and stillness of the small hamlet of Findeln, eating at the Findlerhof or Enzian, which is a cosy half-hidden haunt popular with the locals. Chez Vrony had a big terrace, hearty food and was decorated inside with art by local Heinz Julen; Fluhalp served great pasta with live music; and Othmar's Skihütte, found on the way to the village, served delicious cakes and Alaskan salmon.

The other good news is that supping in town isn't as expensive as its reputation suggests. While children may be happy with their favourite spag-bol every night, the fantastic Seiler-Pass dine-around programme offers an inclusive table d'hôte menu in thirteen restaurants around Zermatt; it's excellent value and means you never have to eat in the same place twice.

For a really great evening, the Hotel Silvana at Furi lets you use their spa before dinner (go either directly from the slopes or you can take the cable car) followed by a scrumptious fondue dinner and then a sled ride all the way back down to the village.

Family activities aren't limited to skiing. There are cheese-making demonstrations; free ice skating on the rink in the middle of town; snowshoe touring; tobogganing between Rotenboden and Riffelberg – where you can hire a sled and let the train take you up to the start as many times as you want; an Ice Palace full of ice sculptures; and heli-touring over the glaciers and around the Matterhorn.

The week ended on a high. Parents and children assembled for a race finale opposite the face of the Matterhorn to the sound of yodelling and cowbells. As they showed off their newfound skills I cheered, we'd cracked the skiing dilemma and enjoyed one of the great natural wonders of the world all in one go.

above **Take your pick of Zermatt's scenically stunning mountain restaurants**

right **You're never too young to start skiing**

IDEAL AGE: 3–16

Powder Byrne International Ltd
250 Upper Richmond Road,
London SW15 6TG, UK
Tel +44 (0) 20 8246 5300
www.powderbyrne.com

Prices on request

ADVENTURES IN LAPLAND

Ice Hotel, Sweden

A five-day adventure to Lapland is something every child, however grown up, dreams of doing. So when the well-known adventure specialists Explore compiled a number of family friendly journeys, specifically designed around children, we just had to go and chill.

Arriving at Stockholm Arlanda Airport is like touching down at Ikea central – crisp, clean, open space, wrapped in glass, with none of the normal stuffy airport air. From Stockholm the ninety-minute flight to Kiruna flies over a billion fir trees cloaked in snow. From the sky, even on the sunniest of days, the giant carpet of frozen brash looks like a shattered black and white negative. It's a wilderness of ice, snow and frozen lakes. The plane touched down onto a deep layer of ice and snow, 200 kilometres inside the Arctic Circle. So remote you wonder what possible reason for populace could exist.

The snow-capped stepped mountains of a massive iron ore mine dominate the landscape like an ice-age Mayan pyramid. Kiruna is best described as a functional industrial town with a sort of Wild West last frontier feel. The traditional buildings are outnumbered by corrugated iron prefabs and huge wind turbines. While the tourist trade has experienced massive growth since the nearby

Icehotel was built in 1992, it can't compete with the 75,000 tonnes of ore mined every day. The shafts are slowly edging their way towards the town, which will have to be completely resettled within twenty years.

The Hotel Kebne (home for three nights) is a comfortable resting place of the prefab variety. You won't see much of it though. The whole trip is characterised by an exciting smorgasbord of outdoor adventure: dog sledding with Arctic huskies, reindeer racing, ice fishing, snowshoeing, abseiling, ice sculpting, moose tracking, thrilling snowmobile safaris and cross-country skiing.

One of the highlights of the tour is the visit to the Sami reindeer herdsman. Locally born Nels Anders saddled up two reindeer with fur-lined sleds – as we hopped on he instructed us to, 'forget your husband, mother, and daughter and just hang on.' We were hastily thrown a rope and sped off hanging on for dear life. 'Bark like a dog,' he yelled as we slowed around the bend, it did the job; the reindeer went straight into fifth gear. After haring round the course we fed the bolder deer a curious diet of sacks of fresh lichen and lingonberries – reindeer steak has to be the most organic meat in the world.

Forget your husband, mother, and daughter and just hang on

The dog sledding was equally thrilling. Seventy silky coated, blue-eyed huskies in an assortment of kennels and pounds howled with excitement – it was 'walkies' time. A licking frenzy started when my daughter popped her hand through the mesh, wagging tails and a general air of eager anticipation prevailed. Twelve dogs were harnessed, linked two-by-two. Within seconds the howling gave way to a peaceful swish and panting of hounds, as they heaved their cargo of four people per sled through the wilderness, up and down the slopes, every husky striving to be top dog.

The optional snowmobiling excursion was something all the children were longing for – kitted out in the all-in-one gortex suits, boots, mitts, helmet and goggles and shown a few simple instructions and we were off on our four-star Polaris skidoos (parent in front, child behind). Pounding across the lake, up through the tundra cutting a path through the virgin snow towards the hills. The snowmobiles are fast, fun and surprisingly quiet. We followed our guide in single line format, snaking our way across spectacular countryside. Halfway up we paused to take in the view of nearby Kiruna and the far-reaching mountains to the north. While parents gazed, the children fell into the thigh-deep snow prompting a snowball fight and snowman competition.

After circumnavigating the lake we raced back to home base – the Icehotel – at full pelt, exhausted but smiling.

On cold clear nights from December to March the Aurora Borealis, or Northern Lights, streak across the northern skyline like a winter greeting from the sun. Normally bluey-green in colour, they create traces like the blood of a wounded dragon. It's not wizardry. They appear when charged electrons from outer space encounter the atmosphere surrounding the Earth and their moving energy is converted into light. It's a wonder of the world that will stay with you forever.

The unforgettable Icehotel

The grand finale of the trip is a night at the Icehotel. Each year farmers equipped with tractors and special saws harvest huge blocks of ice from the River Torne. Snow cannons transform the river by fusing the water with air to form a mixture known as 'snis' – hard as cement, it both insulates and protects from the sun's rays thus prolonging the hotel's life. But the waters are only on loan. In May the whole structure melts back into the river – respectfully returned to its source, only to be re-incarnated the following winter. There's something poetic about its cycle, man so often eclipses nature, here its annual sequence is a celebration of nature's supremacy.

In this part of the world, knowledge about snow and ice has always been a necessity. The Samis have over 300 words for snow (we could only think of ten: ice, snow, sleet, slush, hail, brash, icicles, icebergs, glacier and igloo). The hotel's initial impact is slightly disconcerting. A 'normal' timber reception hall leads down to long ice corridors passing wooden chalets – there's nothing very special about it. Then two reindeer-coated doors with antlers for handles open and the transformation from the mundane to the fantastic is instantaneous. An ice palace with an ice-crystal chandelier, ice beds, glassy furniture and ice sculpture. By day it's an ice museum open to the general public for a small fee, but from six o'clock it's a residents' only domain. Each of the dramatically different suites is designed by artists from around the world ranging from fabulous to pure fetish – we chose a suite resembling an avalanche of giant snowballs designed by Australians Daniel Rosenbaum and Dylan Pillemer.

You'll eat well during your stay. 'Wild is wonderful' said the Icehotel's chef Jens Seitovaara, 'I find my inspiration in nature's own mix of colours and flavours.' He likes to compose his menus like a symphony, always searching for the ultimate harmonies and contrasts. Air-dried moose filet, ptarmigan, reindeer and Arctic char form the staple diet in these climes.

People frequently ask whether it's really possible to sleep in temperatures of -5°C; last year, in its short four-month life, 15,000 people did just that, but for those preferring traditional accommodation, cosy cabins are a welcome alternative. The Icehotel has been such a success it has opened numerous icebars in various cities around the world. Colourful vodka-based cocktails served in ice-carved glasses cause no end of high spirits in the original Absolut Icebar providing a bit of Dutch courage before heading off to your fur lined icebed for the night. Most of us found sleeping in a giant igloo surprisingly comfortable, however, we were very grateful to thaw out in the sauna and steaming showers first thing. Do it again? You bet we would.

Icy interiors of the spectacular Icehotel

TIP
• *March is the best month to visit, the temperatures are warmer, the days longer and there is a very good chance of seeing the Aurora Borealis (Northern Lights) on clear, cold nights*

IDEAL AGE: 10–16

Explore Worldwide Ltd, Nelson House, 55 Victoria Road, Farnborough, Hampshire GU14 7PA, UK
Tel +44 (0) 870 333 4001
www.explore.co.uk

Arctic Ice Adventure from £845 per adult and from £704 per child (eleven years and under) plus a kitty of £110 for five days
Minimum age five

TO BOARD OR NOT TO BOARD?

Tschuggen Grand Hotel, Switzerland

Where better for a family to learn to snowboard than Arosa on the host slopes to the 2007 World Snowboard Championships? As the girl in the tourist office told us, 'You might even have a champion as your instructor'. Arosa's gentle slopes, predominantly blues and reds, are perfect for beginners and popular with families. Plus its high altitude (1,800 metres) and location in a mountain bowl surrounded by a ring of peaks, means it's guaranteed snow from November to April. All in all, a promising start.

Full of optimism, we convened at the base of the nursery slope for classes with the Swiss Ski School. Without doubt, quicker progress can be achieved with one-to-one tuition but the camaraderie and fun elements of group lessons make them preferable for most children.

An uphill start

Our first day on the slopes was not all plain sailing. Having started with eight in the class, by four o'clock we were already down to three. Casualty number one came courtesy of a particularly nasty fall, face down into the piste, resulting in a bleeding nose. The quick demo on how to fall on your elbows, not your wrists, obviously had not had time to sink in? It was wrists out and bam into the ice. Victim number two actually had her chin sliced wide open by a wayward board and was rushed off to the doctor for stitches. One smashed knee later and two others decided they'd seen enough; it was time to retire before the contagious track record for injuries claimed another victim.

We were left to ponder just how much of boarding is down to natural ability and how much is in the mind. 'Get in the zone', I kept telling myself only to hear something stronger yelling, 'what on earth do I want to do this for anyway?' It's estimated that you'll fall over twenty times an hour as a beginner and unless you can perfect your falling technique, the chances of injury, however slight, are huge. Too huge for me I'm afraid. Being the wrong side of forty had me reaching for my unyielding ski boots with unnatural verve. The instinct for self-preservation far outweighed any daredevilry.

It became apparent that we at least had one natural snowboarder in the family. Isabella, our middle daughter, was proving to have real flair for the sport. Maybe you're just born a boarder. Her two sisters, however, had had enough and jumped at the offer to swap their cumbersome snowboards for skis.

Isabella, our middle daughter, was proving to have real flair for the sport

Staying on board

Day two and we awoke to dream-worthy skiing conditions; a smattering of soft powder, temperatures around 2°C and clear, blue skies. On days like this there is only place to be on this planet – in the mountains. What's more, while not all of the runs were open, the pistes were deserted. The third week in December is too early in the season for most holiday-makers and Swiss children are still at school.

With daughters one and three happily re-deployed in ski school, we spent two hours exploring the terrain.

From the summit of the Weisshorn you could clearly see whispers of smoky clouds snaking through the valley. Icicles the length of organ pipes hung from wooden huts and animal tracks crisscrossed the peaks. While the rest of Europe had ground to a halt due to freezing fog, we had 20:20 vision across the summits.

The days zoomed by in quick succession; each brought uncustomary cloudless skies and warmth. And we were making steady progress. By day five, some quite accomplished boarding – and skiing – was appearing.

opposite and above
The stunning Tschuggen Spa

Twenty-first century spa

Home was this season's hottest new property the Tschuggen Grand Hotel and Bergoase Spa, prominently located at the base of the south-eastern slopes. For those who like to ski from dawn until dusk the main thing to shout about is the long-awaited Tschuggen Coaster. The first of its kind in the world, this futuristic transport system connects the hotel to the heart of Arosa's ski slopes by means of nine-seater pods – whizzing you from lobby to slopes in minutes. No more queues; no more cold.

The spa, equally twenty-first century, is linked to the hotel by a dramatic glass bridge. Spread over four floors and 3,500 square metres in size, it uses light and space to soothe away the trauma of your bumps and bruises. In this world of wellness, the hardest decision is whether to ski or spa, whether you're four or forty.

There were things we loved about Arosa: the people, the food and the efficient bus company – which even returned our daughter's lost gloves to the hotel. And a couple of things we weren't so keen on, like charging for tap water in the surprisingly smoky restaurants.

As for the boarding, well, one out of five probably isn't bad. Families skiing together are two-a-penny; families boarding together are not. The fact that you need stomach muscles of steel, knees like springs and the determination of an ox may have something to do with it.

left **Arosa panorama**

IDEAL AGE: 3–16

Tschuggen Grand Hotel, Sonnenbergstrasse CH-7050, Arosa, Switzerland
Tel +41 (0) 81 378 99 99
www.tschuggen.ch/en/

130 rooms
Double rooms from £241 a night
Opens for the ski season from December until April

Hotel kindergarten for children from three years old, open daily 9.00 am – 12.00 pm and 4.00 pm – 8.00 pm.
Young Generation Club for children from twelve years upwards. Various ski clubs are available at this resort

THE REAL DEAL

Club Med Peisey-Vallandry, France

Club Med. What image do those two words conjure up for you? Could it be the French equivalent to the Butlins-style holiday village beset by forced camaraderie, mediocre food and thousands of children? Or could it be the fantastic, all-inclusive holiday option with unlimited possibilities for fun and friendship, all wrapped up at a very reasonable price? In the past I've fallen unquestioningly into the first category, never tempted to think otherwise – until I heard tell that Club Med was raising its game with a rolling programme of refurbishments and new builds in a bid to redefine its image and shift upmarket.

The one that caught my eye was the 'holiday village', which opened last season in Peisey-Vallandry, midway between Les Arcs and La Plagne in the French Alps. It looked the perfect spot to launch my new career as a snowboarder – a skill I planned to master in conjunction with my thirteen-year-old son, Felix. He was to be the grungy schoolboy on that inevitable rite of passage between skiing and snowboarding and I was to be the sad forty-one-year-old mother, desperately unwilling to accept the limitations of either age or fitness.

There are many praises I could sing about Club Med Peisey-Vallandry – the sharp, contemporary design of its bedrooms and bar area, the sheer quality and quantity of food, and the boundless enthusiasm of its staff, to name but three – but it's the all-inclusive nature of the Club Med package that cuts the real deal. The price you pay includes travel costs, accommodation, three eat-as-much-as-you-want meals a day, all alcoholic and non-alcoholic drinks (except Champagne), ski passes, ski hire and, crucially, all-day tuition for those who want it with ESF instructors on loan to Club Med for the season.

Sticking it out the whole day

Every age group and every ability is catered for, and skiing and snowboarding are both on offer. Each class returns to the hotel everyday at lunchtime so guests can choose on a daily basis whether they just attend the morning class, get back out there for the afternoon class or stick it out the whole day. Kids aged eight to twelve can sign themselves in and out of the Juniors Club and teenagers are treated like grown-ups. It's a great set up.

In our snowboarding group Felix and I had a mixed bag of fellow beginners including a couple of slightly older English teenagers and various adults, one or two of whom weren't far from me in age. In charge of us was Francois, barely more than a teenager

Every age group and every ability is catered for, and skiing and snowboarding are both on offer

above and opposite **There's fun for all ages at Peisey-Vallandry**

himself, who took one look at me and rolled his eyes to the heavens.

No, I'm not large or ungainly. Neither am I unfit. But I do believe in safety, hence I was armed as if for combat – black crash helmet, wrap-around shades, wrist pads and ski pants with fully padded knees. Felix was similarly attired – hardly the image of cutting-edge, teenage cool – but he didn't care. On one of my more spectacular falls, when my head took the full force of an icy piste, I blessed that helmet, and without those wrist pads I would have ended up in casualty.

We level-pegged it through the first day, mother and son, side-by-side trying to get to grips with the snowboarder's shuffle (walking with one foot strapped to the board and one foot free) and the arduous task of getting on and off chairlifts, but thereafter the talent gap began to widen and the twenty-eight years between us became ever more apparent. Felix, unafraid of falling over, perfectly balanced and unperturbed by leaning backwards started to look like a real snowboarder. I floundered. With each fall another part of my body began to hurt, my shoulders ached from pushing myself up from the ground and my confidence plummeted.

I learned how to slip from side to side, facing forwards on my snowboard, but I never learned how to

We level-pegged it through the first day, mother and son, side-by-side trying to get to grips with the snowboarder's shuffle

opposite and above **Peisey-Vallandry holiday village**

turn – every instinct screaming in terror at the prospect of leaning backwards while going downhill. Felix, meanwhile, graduated from falling-over snowboarder to smooth easy rider within three or four days. He was living proof of all those things us adults know in our hearts to be true about the young – they have no fear, their muscles are stretchy and their bodies limber. They absorb information and master skills with consummate ease and make physical challenges look simple. By the fourth day, as a tear-stained heap of bruised bones and aching muscles I resigned from snowboarding school and checked into Club Med's spa to coax my body back to life.

Felix resigned shortly afterwards, not out of failure but triumph. He was simply too good for the rest of the pack – a bullet in black who could keep up with any skier and take on any terrain. For my part I can say quite happily that I shall never stand on a snowboard again. But Club Med Peisey-Vallandry – now that I would say yes to.

> The young have no fear, their muscles are stretchy and their bodies limber

IDEAL AGE: 4–16

Club Med, Peisey-Vallandry, France
Club Med Travel, 25 Henrietta Street, London WC2E 8NA
Tel + 44 (0) 8453 675747
www.clubmed.co.uk

280 rooms
Prices from £939 per person per week including flights from the UK, transfers, accommodation, all meals, ski classes, passes, equipment hire and kids' club

Mini Club Med for children aged four to ten, Junior Club Med for children aged eleven to seventeen, open six days a week, 8.30 a.m. – 9.00 p.m.
The village welcomes children from four months old

SKI CATS FOR SCAREDY CATS

Jackson Hole, Wyoming, USA

I'm sorry, but you just don't go to Jackson Hole, Wyoming, unless you plan to be brave enough to try something new, even if you consider yourself an intermediate scaredy cat, like me. After all, this is the Wild West; where plenty of ski instructors ditch the bobble for a cowboy hat, and the real McCoy still wear holsters in the grocery store. Jackson Hole has the most challenging terrain of any ski resort in the US, fifty per cent of its runs are expert, and the instructors live to push you 'out of your comfort zone'. With a mountain called the Big One offering the longest vertical drop of any American resort (4,000 feet), a unique open gates boundary policy that gives skiers and snowboarders 3,000 square acres of backcountry to explore, the place buzzes with bravery. That is until this mother and her nine-year-old son arrived in January, shaking at the knees.

The purpose of our trip was a mother-and-son bonding exercise, with my mission to ski powder for the first time and my son's to try snowboarding. We had chosen America because European skiers were picking daisies on the top of mountains when we booked in December, and we needed some of the guaranteed eleven metres of snow that packs the slopes of the Teton Mountains every year.

My son Humphrey rolled up, rather than enrolled, at the Kids Ranch on day one, and was quickly moved through his paces. A keen skateboarder, he was in a snowboarding beginners group with his ten-year-old friend Ned, an expert skier. Much emphasis was put on safety and helmet wearing, but the group fall-out rate from injury was frighteningly high. By the end of each day it seemed only Ned and Humphrey were there to exchange knuckle high fives with their instructor and be praised as 'awesome rippers, dudes'. Snowboarding effortlessly weeds out the wannabes from the willbes, and the boys had a cowboy swagger for being the only group survivors at the end of the week, taking the blue runs by day two.

On the morning of the Snow Cat trip from Togwotee Lodge, a blizzard blew in, and the talk in our 'condo' in Teton Village was all about the eighteen inches of powder expected by the end of the day. Our group of twelve huddled by an open fire, and listened open mouthed to a terrifying avalanche safety talk. 'We are skiing backcountry here', said our guide 'Shoveller'. 'There are no groomed runs, and if you hear a cracking sound, you need to ski off at a forty-five degree angle'. I had a panic attack. By the time Shoveller made us all stand up and imitate him putting

This is the Wild West; where plenty of ski instructors ditch the bobble for a cowboy hat

his arm in front of his mouth, waving his elbow up and down to make an air pocket to breathe under an avalanche, I could barely hear his words above my beating heart.

On the Snow Cat's slow chug up the mountain, inside what felt like a shipping container, an American Buddhist doctor called David became my guru. He suggested that I established my mindset as 'Beyond hope and fear' and offered the mantra, 'I can ski powder' to repeat endlessly. It didn't work. I resorted to yoga breath work ('breathe in Hope, breathe out Fear') to reduce my hyperventilation, and when Shoveller clanked open the door at the top of the mountain, and shouted 'Welcome to the white room', I was ready for death.

Into the whiteout

Stepping into the blizzard at the top of the mountain was like passing through the back of the wardrobe into Narnia. There was a shimmering light as the snow caught the sun, and we were all shadowy silhouettes as we set off down the mountain to get out of the wind, now hitting us at a factor of -15°C. We regrouped by trees waiting for the go-ahead from the pathfinder in front, and the word came back through the radio. 'I've heard a crack over this side,' confirmed the guide, 'so tell everyone to ski the other side of the trees'.

As we set off, ten seconds apart, I fell almost immediately out of fear. With my first fall I learnt an enduring lesson of the day – it doesn't hurt. Falling into powder is like flopping onto a duck down feather duvet, the mountain catches you in a marshmallow embrace. Suddenly my fear evaporated and I became liberated by the freedom of falling down, like a child rolling down the hill. It wasn't the same whooping fun that everyone else was having, whizzing past me, but it was fun all the same.

By three o'clock, after five hours on the mountain, with lunch being a sandwich eaten as we slowly cranked up to the next virgin site, I was exhausted. Powder skiing was different from skiing groomed runs, whatever anyone had said, and the whole new dance, like the Texan Two-Step we had tried out in

left **Local condo and ranger**
opposite **Ready, Steady, Go**

the Million Dollar Cowboy Bar, was making my muscles ache. My mind began to play tricks. 'What if my last run is … exactly that … my last run'? 'Perhaps I should quit while I am ahead?' I appealed to Shoveller for a reprieve on the final fling.

'No way,' he replied. 'You are going to do it, you are going to be fine, and I'm going to be right behind you. All you have to do is to keep breathing, because you need oxygen to those legs.' To breathe was the best advice I'd been given, and finally, on the last run, I floated down the mountain on top of the snow without a wipe out. 'Yee-ha!' I whooped at the bottom. I was intoxicated. Shoveller swooped in behind me. 'How much fun was that!' he shouted to the group. 'If that wasn't some of the best powder that y'all ever skied, then you must be powder snobs!'

Well I wasn't until my trip to Jackson Hole. But I am now.

Stepping into the blizzard at the top of the mountain was like passing through the back of the wardrobe into Narnia

IDEAL AGE: 3–16

Togwotee Mountain Lodge, PO Box 91, Moran, Wyoming 83013, USA
Tel +1 800 543 2847
www.togwoteelodge.com

35 rooms
Full day (seven to ten runs) Cat Skiing at Togwotee Lodge, including lunch and transportation from Jackson Hole from US$369

Rudolph
Cupid
Dancer
Blitzen
Prancer
Donner
Comet
Dasher
Vixen

SANTA SPECIAL

Lapland, Finland

'Dasher and Dancer, Prancer and Blitzen, Comet and Cupid, Donner and Vixen', sang the children on the way to the airport. Even though it was four in the morning, they couldn't believe their luck – they were off to find Rudolph and Father Christmas… in Lapland.

We knew it was going to be a different kind of day the second we were met at the airport by life-sized Hal the husky, Rudi the reindeer and a collection of fairies and elfin helpers who had festooned the check-in staff in Santa-hats and tinsel.

The three-hour flight to Kittila, deep in Finland's Arctic Circle whizzed past as the excited captives were kept entertained with carols and Christmas tunes. Once at Kittila it was straight into the clothing shed to collect pre-ordered Arctic clothing. Designated sacks containing waterproof boots and insulated ski-suits were efficiently handed out to each family. We were reminded that wrapping up warm is essential as temperatures regularly drop as low as -20 °C.

Split into several groups, there was just enough time for a quick snowball fight in the car park before boarding the coaches for the twenty-minute drive to Levi. First up was a traditional husky dog sled ride through the forest, followed by a snowmobile adventure over bumps and mounds across the tundra. Babies and tots too small to straddle the seats were towed in fur-lined sleds as dads revved the handlebars and sped off James Bond style. At the finish line an open fire and steaming cups of delicious lingonberry juice warmed everyone's hands and stomachs before setting off again.

It was only two in the afternoon but already dusk had set in and flickering lanterns lit the path towards the toboggan slope and reindeer track. After squeals of giggles and a few near collisions on the plastic toboggans, local Sami dressed in national costume led us to their reindeer sleighs. Shy little deer obediently pulled families through the woods as snow dropped from the frozen boughs of the fir trees.

With everything happening in such rapid succession there was no time for anything but excitement and gleeful expectation of what was next. Children were continually instructed to keep their eyes open for magic Tinkerbell dust, elves or even Santa himself. Wondering if it could really make them fly, youngsters greedily ate handfuls of fresh powder snow.

After three hours packed with activities it was time for a rest and some lunch. Up the hill, past the illuminated ski-slopes where international competitors were warming up for a race, we arrived at Levi for a

Children were continually instructed to keep their eyes open for magic Tinkerbell dust, elves or even Santa himself

buffet of pizza, pasta and salad. Although still early afternoon it was pitch black outside. On a clear bright morning you can see as far as Sweden and Russia we were told; we were hoping for a clear sky and a chance to spot the regularly visible and spectacular Northern Lights.

Where, oh where is Santa?

Once nourished and refreshed it was time to visit Santa's village. The children stepped into the workshop eagerly eying the gifts being wrapped by some of the elves, while others were sanding down wooden toys – a make-believe factory in action. Outside, more of Santa's helpers were whizzing pre-schoolers around on chairs-cum-sleds between the cabins and twinkling trees. The frosted wooden pen held none other than the nine famous reindeer. The shiny-coated Prancer came to nose at the little faces as they peered through the slats and posed wide-eyed for photos.

In the post office elves were busy sorting letters sent to Father Christmas from children all over the world. While some children wrote their Christmas lists, we crept upstairs to see a sleeping elf, who smiled sweetly as she lay cosily tucked up in her bunk bed. It was utterly entrancing for the children and a delightful second-childhood experience for parents.

But where, oh where was Santa? The children had been waiting all day for one particular moment. Quietly and discreetly families were siphoned off for a special audience. The benevolent white-bearded old man sat in the corner next to an enormous pile of presents. Peering over his glasses he smiled at the children as he passed them a gift and wished them 'Happy Christmas'. For the children, overcome with awe and expectation, the moment was perfectly short and very sweet.

The plane home was almost silent. Sleepy heads dreaming of a wonderland where magic is real and dreams come true.

left **Scenes from Santa's village**
above right **Jingle bells on a husky sled ride**

IDEAL AGE: 3–8

Cosmos Holidays, Dale House, Tiviot Dale, Stockport, Cheshire SK1 1TB
Tel + 44 (0) 871 4238422
www.cosmos.co.uk

Prices on request
I booked my trip through Cosmos who first started taking people to see Santa in Lapland twenty years ago. But there are now several operators organising such trips and providing a wide variety of choices. For a list of those operators contact www.holidaysfromheaven.com

TIPS

• *This is an ideal trip for under-fives who still believe in Father Christmas*
• *Clothing and shoe sizes for Arctic protection-wear will be taken when you book your tickets*
• *Remember to take your Christmas present list for Father Christmas, warm hats and gloves, and snacks to keep you going*
• *Be aware that this is a very long day and includes two lengthy flights. However, if appropriate your trip can be extended with overnight accommodation and further activities*

OLYMPIC ODYSSEY

Vancouver and Whistler, Canada

For the last ten years Whistler, in Canada's western state of British Columbia, has frequently been acclaimed as the world's number one ski resort with an enviable reputation for thigh-deep powder, phenomenal scenery and the perfect arena for child-friendly classes. Last year its supremacy was made official: it will host the 2010 Winter Olympics.

Conveniently lying next to Vancouver, one of the world's pre-eminent outdoor-lifestyle cities – along with the likes of Cape Town and Sydney – this trip offers a double-whammy appeal for a culture-cum-countryside holiday. It would be sinful to travel halfway round the globe and miss out on Vancouver's plethora of family-orientated attractions – I can think of few destinations so generous with their entertainment.

Within minutes of arriving at Fairmont's downtown waterfront property, you can enjoy 'walkies' with the sweet-natured hotel Labrador Holly, who knows her way around the block, as children take turns at being shown around the Pan Pacific Seawall. In the morning you awake to the novel sight of seaplanes landing in the harbour below. A swim in the steaming outdoor pool, followed by towers of delicious maple syrup waffles, and you're ready for an action-packed day.

First stop is Stanley Park's aquarium, where feeding the resident sea otters handfuls of clam strings or communing with the adorable Beluga whales is the definite order of the day. From here it's a quick hop across the Lions Gate Bridge to the city's number one attraction – the swaying wooden Capilano Suspension Bridge. Once over the canyon and safely on the ridge, children and adults alike run across the trail of suspended walkways, stopping to hug 'Doug' or 'Grandma Capilano', the 500-year-old, sixty-metre fir trees that appear to touch the sky.

Every city in the world should have a Storyeum – where interactive history is brought to life. The trip starts in a giant barrel-shaped lift that moves gently down into the bowels of the city's picturesque Gastown. Ten metres below ground level, you step out into a vast world of interconnecting themed theatre sets, with actors depicting a chronology of various historical events. You follow a personal trail of the lives that have shaped Canada as you gather round a fire with the First Nations Indians, sail the high seas with the arrival of the British and Spanish explorers, hit the gold rush in Bakersville, and experience the ambitious reality of the building of the Trans-Canadian railway. Don't miss it.

A swim in the steaming outdoor pool, followed by towers of delicious maple syrup waffles

previous page **Fairmont Chateau Whistler**   above **Alaskan husky racing**   opposite **Relax in the Four Seasons' fire and ice splendour**

You can go dog-
sledding with a
team of Alaskan
racing huskies

Another fun-filled day starts with the hop-on hop-off trolley bus ride to Granville Island market, from where it's fun to take the aqua bus to the amazing Scienceworld, where the Eureka Zone is a haven of educational fun for all ages. There is so much to do that any thoughts of jetlag are completely forgotten, and whether you have two days or two weeks the city promises not to disappoint.

The Sea to Sky Highway
From Vancouver, the journey up to Whistler is a dramatic ninety-minute drive along the aptly named, eye-catching Sea to Sky Highway. Up until last year,

if you said you were skiing in Whistler you'd be asked almost rhetorically, 'Are you staying at the Chateau?' Now there's a new contender on the block. While the neo-gothic Chateau triumphs with its unbeatable ski-to-your-door location resting majestically at the foot of the nursery slopes, the new Four Seasons wins hands down on bedroom size and contemporary fire and ice decor, with each room a minimum forty-eight square metres. Both hotels have fabulous spas with outdoor pools and an extensive menu of feel well, look well, live well treatments. Special welcome treats of teddy bears on skis, miniature cookies and a kids' newsletter make little VIPs feel very at home indeed.

One of the joys of Whistler is the food. Both the Chateau's Wildflower restaurant and the Four Seasons' 52 80 bistro offer inventive and sophisticated dishes, and are exceptionally child-friendly. For something a little different, try the giant Percheron horse-drawn sleigh ride followed by a four-course gourmet fondue dinner. Surprisingly, there's little choice in venue for mountain dining, which is quantity rather than quality biased but refreshingly inexpensive for Europeans who have become used to paying top dollar.

If you don't want to ski every day, don't worry. You can go dogsledding with a team of Alaskan racing huskies, snowmobiling, zip-wiring, treetop-walking or on snowshoe adventures – or simply wander round the shops and restaurants. If it is the skiing you're after, statistics alone will give you confidence: three glaciers, 200 trails, twelve alpine bowls, the longest run seven miles, average snowfall nine metres with a ski season that runs from November to August.

Whistler is in fact a twin resort spread between two mountains offering an awesome quantity of skiing. Blackcomb Mountain offers more sheltered skiing, while Whistler Mountain has earned its reputation for deep powder but is more exposed. Both have equally breathtaking panoramas with immaculately groomed pistes and no queues. The names of the pistes

above **Whistler street scene**

will cause much amusement. At the end of a day's ski-ing you can zoom down Freefall on to Grub Stake and carefully past School Marm, meeting your little ones on the Yellow Brick Road.

Impressive mountain hosts

Whistler Kids is a well-run, professional ski school where children quickly settle in and eagerly progress from level to level. The adult class was the best I've experienced anywhere, and my twenty-year-old instructor had me bombing down black mogul fields that I would never have dreamt of tackling.

The Canadians are impressive mountain hosts. Every day volunteer ski guides offer a free ninety-minute orientation tour for intermediate and advanced skiers, pointing out sights of interest as you whizz around the best prepared slopes – it's worth getting the inside info. Your creature comforts are also taken seriously. Tissue dispensers, known as sniffle stations, and giant hairdryers to warm your boots during a hot-chocolate break are all part of Whistler's de rigueur service. After a couple of days the friendliest

above **Winter wonderland**

ski-lift staff in the world even recognise the children and greet them by name.

Intrawest, the designers and managers of Whistler, know they've created a winner and are already copying the blueprint, generating new resorts around the world. All in all, Whistler has a justifiable magic that leaves you wondering: where next?

IDEAL AGE: 3–16

For family-friendly holidays to Vancouver and Whistler contact www.holidaysfromheaven.com
Tel + 44 (0) 118 933 3777
www.fourseasons.com
www.fairmont.com

Ski school operates from 8.30 a.m. – 3.30 p.m.

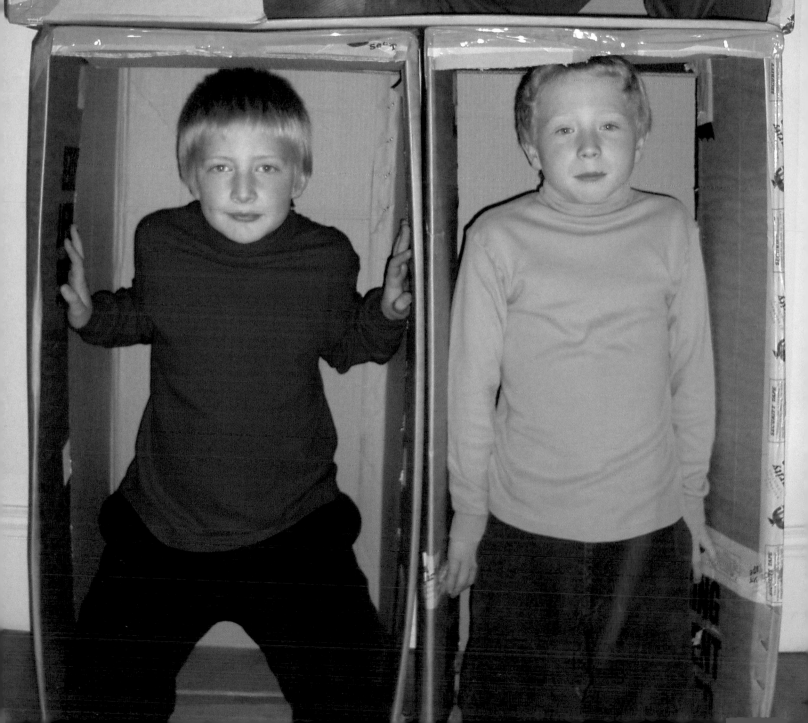
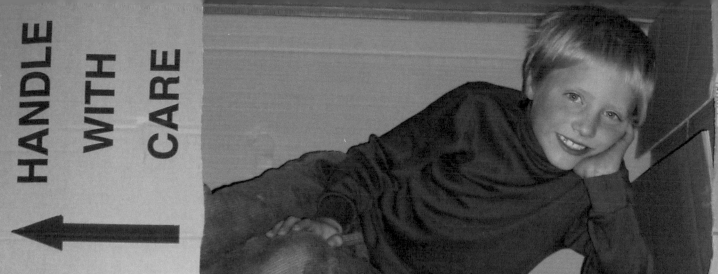

HOW TO TRAVEL WITH KIDS

www.holidaysfromheaven.com

The rule of thumb when travelling with small children is that 'getting there' is far harder than 'being there'. The more thought I have put into how to travel with my three in tow – often an equation between the age of the child and the distance to travel – the easier the holiday has been. One mother noted that, 'my twins flew on our laps across Europe to Greece without a sound. At two years old, I would strap them into a familiar car seat and drive them across the Continent to avoid departure lounges. When toddlers, with airlines insisting on keeping everyone in their seats at all times and making legroom a thing of a past, a trip on Eurostar – during which a walk up and down the corridor would keep the children happier than being told to belt up at the back – always proved to be a better bet.'

To help you prepare for the necessary evil of taking the tribe across the globe, we have compiled the following list of dos and don'ts. The list begins with the not-so-obvious suggestion of talking to the customer services department of your chosen airline before flying out. Without you knowing it, many airlines and tour operators do offer families special provision to pre-book seats together, or – in the case of BA for example – to order a healthy child's meal online, or book one of their special Britax child seats on board.

As someone who has experienced the horror of boarding a plane to find the baby change bag had been left on the back seat of the car, I would argue that paying a little extra for a decent airline is worth its weight in nappy bags.

Finally, what rings true for a mother of a baby, will not necessarily register on the Richter scale for a mother with a pre-schooler. For this reason, we have divided up the list of dos and don'ts to cover the most difficult ages. After the age of six, when the wonderful world of books, Game Boys, iPods and in-car/flight entertainment kick in, you are on your own – free to open a book and read yourself, perhaps for the first time that year.

From hard experience, it is also better to travel pessimistically than optimistically. Having suffered a delay on a trip to Spain on my own with a bored eighteen-month-old son who seemed intent on clearing the bottles and packets from the bottom shelf of Boots and diving into the Disney Store's pile of Pooh Bears, I later became obsessed with checking what airport authorities provided in the way of a 'family' area once parents had checked in. Copenhagen airport, for example, has a fabulous replica of an airplane with peekaboo windows, a slide down the back and endless tables of Lego for small children to play on. Some terminals in Heathrow, however, have nothing but shops and won't even let you sit at the oyster bar for a restorative glass of wine if you have a child in tow.

Again, preparation can be the key. A quick look at the Internet or a call to the airport before you book might make you choose a regional airport rather than Gatwick or Heathrow, because with little ones size does matter. Little things please little minds, and when it comes to travelling with kids, bigger is not always better.

Kids' clubs

There are no universal regulations for kids' clubs in hotels so standards do vary depending on your destination and your hotel. Clubs should offer a safe and stimulating play environment and provide activities that appeal to and inspire children, regardless of the length or frequency of their visits. If they are biased towards the local area, so much the better.

The following checklist is not a comprehensive tick-the-box guide, but should give you enough basic information to assess the club's suitability depending on the age of your children.

Checklist

· How safe is the environment? Gleneagles, for example, has an ingenious tagging system, like a clothing security device, for keeping track of children
· How engaging is it for children? Do they offer a daily timetable of activities?
· How well managed is the service?
· What is the ratio of staff to children?
· How cheerful, kind and patient are the staff? Ask to meet the team
· Parents should feel welcome to stay with their children if they want to, especially at mealtimes
· Location, location, location: is the club bright and airy or tucked away in a dead-end zone, dark and uninviting?
· What are the resources like? Are staff able to use other areas of the hotel e.g. the ballroom, or the grounds
· Access to fresh air should be a pre-requisite. It's no holiday for a child if they are confined to some chilled air-con pen

The clubs should comply with all relevant Health & Safety legislation, including the screening of Play-Station games, administration of medication, infection control, accident and fire procedures and comprehensive written risk assessments, all of which you are entitled to enquire about if you have any concerns.

Staff should also be suitably trained in first aid, anaphylaxis and have EpiPen training.

Healthy drinks and snacks should be available throughout the day as part of promoting a healthy lifestyle and avoiding dehydration, and you should be asked whether your child has any special dietary requirements or nut allergies.

Staff should interact enthusiastically and purposefully with children in play activities, building their confidence and self-esteem. You should expect an appropriate balance between activities children can choose for themselves and those inspired by adults, which will enable them to plan, negotiate, take decisions and be independent.

Activities

A constantly changing theme in the kids' clubs renews energy for both staff and children. Although the focus is on fun and relaxation rather than learning, activities should ideally feature the local environment. Often kids' clubs' activities are divided into different age groups, but there should be flexibility for the age groups to interact, or for siblings to stay together if they want.

Examples of activities at the best clubs

· Look for novel outdoor activities, such as dog walking at Fairmont Waterfront in Vancouver, hermit crab racing at Reethi Rah in the Maldives or birdwatching at Hell Bay in the Scilly Isles
· A well equipped club, such as Woolley Grange, will have a huge number of props for imaginative play such as dressing-up, a grocery shop, a playhouse with dolls, Brio train set, castles and farmyards, doll's house, ethnic dolls and board games like Snakes and Ladders
· Artistic play is always fun: including T-shirt painting, creating art for the walls, mask making and even weaving with local Rastafarians as offered by Round Hill in Jamaica

In the twenty-first century it is becoming increasingly commonplace for children to be an inclusive part of guest hospitality. Although you don't expect to see signs saying, 'Only well behaved children are welcome', it is important to remember to be considerate to other guests who may not have little ones in tow.

DOS AND DON'TS

Babies up to eight months

☺ Do check with the customer services of the airline to find out what provision is made for families with babies. For example, whether you can take a pushchair to the boarding gate, where they are checked into the hold and reclaimed at the other end, either at the aircraft door (ideal) or the carousel (not so ideal). Regulations vary between different airports and airlines.

☺ Do request bulkhead seats if your child is under two, where the cot/child seat is attached after take-off. These seats are often near the loo, and also offer a little more legroom.

☺ Do take all baby essentials as hand luggage – you may get delayed taking off.

☺ Do take a wet flannel in a plastic bag as well as wipes. Babies hate the taste of chemicals on their fingers.

☺ Do feed your baby on take-off and landing to stop discomfort as the cabin pressure changes.

☹ Don't forget to take the food your baby is used to, and ask for it to be warmed. Many airlines do not carry baby food, and on board is not the place to acquaint your baby with new tastes.

☹ Don't plan for your baby to sleep throughout the journey. Even if the baby does sleep, if there is any turbulence, the cabin crew will disturb them so that their seatbelt can be attached, according to regulations.

☹ Don't forget to take your baby's favourite teddy. Airlines do provide sheets and blankets for cots but the familiarity of a teddy can make the difference between sleep and no sleep.

☹ Don't forget to offer frequent feeds, including water, because flying is an especially dehydrating experience for an infant.

Infants aged between nine months and two years

This is the most challenging age, when children are crawling, walking, demanding constant entertainment, and the rest of the passengers tend to scowl rather than coo over your little angels.

☺ Do book airline seats well in advance so you can all sit together, and order children's meals at the same time.

☺ Do take a supply of healthy snacks (rather than sweet ones, which will result in the inevitable sugar rush) such as raisins, bread sticks and rice cakes. Just the conjuror's trick of pulling something new out of the bag will be a distraction for a few minutes.

☺ Do take reins for toddlers. It is often a long walk from the aircraft through passport control to the carousel, and reins can keep a toddler upright.

☺ Do ask if the swimming pool (if there is one) is attended full-time.

☺ Do take daytime flights if you possibly can. Children without the familiar routine of bedtime often do not sleep at all, so neither will you.

☹ Don't forget that although children under two pay ten per cent of the adult fare, they are often provided with no food and no baggage allowance, so check ahead about weight allowance and number of bags admitted. Some airlines, such as BA, do offer twenty-three kilos of luggage allowance for under twos.

☹ Don't be tempted to drug your child with Piriton or Vallergan (over-the-counter and prescription antihistamines sometimes prescribed by doctors for jetlag), unless you are able to try out the medication before flying. It can result in hyperactivity. Camomile tea, on the other hand, is harmless and may bring on sleep.

☹ Don't put off the trip to the loo until landing. Just before descent is normally the ideal time, and prevents a crisis in the long wait to disembark.

Children aged between two and six years

Children at this age usually love the excitement of flying, the main problem is stopping them watching videos for ten hours non-stop, often washed down with the unlimited fizzy drinks that come free from the trolley.

☺ Do put a bracelet tag on your child with your mobile phone number if they are prone to running away in crowds.

☺ Do get your children to pack a small backpack with Lego, magazines and colouring pencils to carry on board. Ask ahead whether entertainment packs are offered.

☺ Do buy one new thing to do with the child as a treat to save for a fractious moment, a new book to read together or a game.

☺ Do remember to take blindfolds if your child will only sleep in the pitch black. A travel pillow may also help to make them comfortable.

☹ Don't forget to have some boiled sweets in your bag to help ears pop on the final descent.

☹ Don't forget to ask at check-in whether you can sit with other families. The best entertainment can be a like-minded child with new magazines and toys in their backpack, and thankful parents looking for respite.

☹ Don't forget to pack the Calpol and a favourite teddy in your hand luggage.

	Pre Bookable Seats	Seats/Cots/Bassinets for Infants	Nappies	Formula	Baby Food	Beakers and Bottles/ other information	In Flight Entertainment Packs	Seat Back TVs/ Entertainment
British Airways	For certain passengers	Limited number of onboard Britax seats which are attached to the bassinet positions, bassinets for infants	No	No	No	On board bottle warming and baby-food warming facilities (only un-opened food in a sealed jar) are available on long haul flights	Themed packs for different ages	Seat back TV/Disney and Cartoon Network and blockbuster movies
Virgin Atlantic	Yes	Sky cots for babies aged up to 12 months. Infant care chairs for infants between 6 and 36 months	Yes	Yes	Yes	Some toilets are fitted with changing facilities and limited spare baby items such as bottles are available	Virgin Atlantic K-ID Pack	Seat back TV/V Kids channels with up to 35 Nintendo games
American Airlines	Yes	Pre bookable wall mounted bassinets are available	No	No	No	Baby bottles can be warmed but are not carried on board	In-flight magazine	Seat back TV only on certain aircraft/ children's films
KLM	No	Bassinets available	No	No	No	Certain baby items are carried on board but you are advised to take your own	Activity packs on intercontinental flights	Seat back TV on certain aircraft/children's films
Air France	No	Sky cots available	No	No	No	Baby bottles can be warmed but are not carried on board	Children receive gifts and toys	No seat back TV
Singapore Airlines	For certain passengers	Sky cots for infants	Yes	Yes	Yes	Disposable bibs, feeding bottles, and baby wipes are available on board	Children's activity packs and toys	Seat back TV/children's cartoons and movies
Qantas	Yes	Bassinets for babies aged up to 18 months	Yes	Yes	Yes	Will warm bottles and have a limited quantity of top brand baby food, milk, baby bottles and brushes, cereals and rusks on board	Children's activity packs	Seat back TV/Wiggles children's programmes
Thai Airways	Yes	Sky cots for infants under 6 months old	No	No	Yes	Baby bottles can be warmed but are not carried on board	No	No seat back TV
Emirates	No	Sky cots are available	No	Yes	Yes	Baby bottles can be warmed but are not carried on board	Children's activity packs	Seat back TV/children's cartoons and movies and computer games
Sri Lankan Airlines	For certain passengers	Sky cots are available	Yes	Yes	Yes	Will warm bottles. Have child care stewardess	Toys and games	Seat back TV/Own movie channel
Gulf Air	Yes	Sky cots are available	Yes	Yes	Yes	Have sky nannies that will arrange everything for you	Activity packs	Seat back TV/Disney Special and kids' movies

Notes: Sky cots are subject to availability and are on a first come first service basis. Nappies, formula milk and food is subject to availability. Certain brands cannot be provided so clients are advised to take their own. Seat back TVs are dependent on the type of aircraft. All other information is subject to change and type of aircraft.

WEATHER TO GO

ᵗ = Average temperature ☀ = Hours of sunshine 💧 = Rain days per month

Argentina
148

	J	F	M	A	M	J	J	A	S	O	N	D
ᵗ	29	28	26	22	19	15	15	17	19	22	25	28
☀	9	9	7	7	5	4	5	6	6	7	8	8
💧	9	8	8	8	7	7	7	7	1	0	9	9

Australia
160

	J	F	M	A	M	J	J	A	S	O	N	D
ᵗ	26	26	24	20	17	14	13	14	16	19	21	24
☀	9	8	7	5	4	4	4	5	6	7	7	8
💧	8	7	10	12	15	15	16	17	15	14	12	10

Canada
234
272

	J	F	M	A	M	J	J	A	S	O	N	D
ᵗ	-5	-1	3	10	16	20	23	22	17	12	3	-3
☀	4	5	6	7	8	9	10	9	7	6	4	3
💧	8	7	9	8	11	13	12	10	9	6	6	7

The Caribbean
50

	J	F	M	A	M	J	J	A	S	O	N	D
ᵗ	28	29	29	30	30	30	30	30	30	30	29	29
☀	8	9	9	9	9	8	9	9	9	8	7	8
💧	10	8	8	7	9	11	14	15	14	15	14	13

China
190

	J	F	M	A	M	J	J	A	S	O	N	D
ᵗ	2	4	11	20	27	31	31	30	26	19	10	3
☀	6	7	8	8	8	8	8	8	7	6	6	
💧	2	3	4	5	9	14	12	7	6	5	2	

Cyprus
40
46

	J	F	M	A	M	J	J	A	S	O	N	D
ᵗ	17	17	19	23	27	30	33	33	31	28	23	19
☀	6	7	8	9	11	12	13	12	11	9	8	6
💧	9	7	5	3	2	1	0	0	1	3	4	8

Czech Republic
166

	J	F	M	A	M	J	J	A	S	O	N	D
ᵗ	1	4	9	14	19	23	24	24	20	14	7	3
☀	2	3	4	6	7	7	7	7	5	4	2	2
💧	14	13	13	12	14	14	14	13	12	13	15	15

Dubai
24
88

	J	F	M	A	M	J	J	A	S	O	N	D
ᵗ	20	21	24	28	33	35	37	38	36	32	27	22
☀	8	8	8	10	12	12	10	10	10	10	9	8
💧	1	2	1	2	0	0	0	0	0	0	1	1

England
76
82
138
144

	J	F	M	A	M	J	J	A	S	O	N	D
ᵗ	7	7	10	13	17	20	22	21	19	15	10	8
☀	2	2	4	5	6	7	6	6	5	3	2	1
💧	17	13	15	14	12	11	12	12	14	14	16	15

Egypt
34

	J	F	M	A	M	J	J	A	S	O	N	D
ᵗ	21	22	24	27	30	33	33	34	32	30	26	23
☀	8	10	10	10	12	13	13	12	1	10	10	9
💧	1	0	1	0	1	0	0	0	0	0	1	1

Finland
268

	J	F	M	A	M	J	J	A	S	O	N	D
ᵗ	-10	-9	-3	3	10	17	19	16	10	3	-3	-7
☀	0	1	3	5	7	9	8	6	3	2	1	0
💧	21	19	16	13	12	13	15	16	17	19	20	20

France: Paris
170

	J	F	M	A	M	J	J	A	S	O	N	D
ᵗ	13	13	15	17	20	24	27	27	25	21	17	13
☀	5	6	6	8	9	10	12	11	9	7	5	5
💧	7	6	6	7	6	3	2	3	6	8	8	7

France: Alps
258

	J	F	M	A	M	J	J	A	S	O	N	D
ᵗ	-4	-4	-3	0	5	8	11	10	8	5	0	-3
☀	4	5	5	5	5	5	6	6	6	6	4	4
💧	16	15	17	19	19	18	19	14	13	13	16	

Greece
116

	J	F	M	A	M	J	J	A	S	O	N	D
ᵗ	16	16	17	21	24	28	29	30	27	24	21	17
☀	3	5	7	8	10	12	13	12	10	6	5	4
💧	11	8	8	4	2	1	0	0	2	5	6	10

India
194

	J	F	M	A	M	J	J	A	S	O	N	D
ᵗ	25	28	34	39	41	40	36	34	35	36	32	27
☀	9	9	9	10	9	7	5	5	6	9	10	9
💧	0	0	0	0	1	2	6	7	3	0	0	0

Ireland
106

	J	F	M	A	M	J	J	A	S	O	N	D
ᵗ	8	8	10	12	15	18	19	19	17	14	10	9
☀	2	3	4	5	6	6	5	5	4	3	2	2
💧	19	15	17	16	15	14	16	16	18	17	18	

Italy
116

	J	F	M	A	M	J	J	A	S	O	N	D
ᵗ	8	10	14	18	23	28	31	30	26	19	13	9
☀	4	5	6	7	9	10	9	7	6	4	4	
💧	9	8	8	9	8	4	6	9	11	9		

Jamaica
56

	J	F	M	A	M	J	J	A	S	O	N	D
ᵗ	29	29	30	30	30	31	32	32	31	31	30	30
☀	7	8	8	7	8	7	8	8	7	6	7	7
💧	9	7	7	7	12	13	14	14	15	17	12	9

Kenya
202
206
218

	J	F	M	A	M	J	J	A	S	O	N	D
ᵗ	31	32	32	31	30	30	29	29	31	32	29	30
☀	9	9	8	8	8	8	7	7	8	7	8	8
💧	8	7	16	16	8	5	5	4	9	18	12	

Mauritius
18

	J	F	M	A	M	J	J	A	S	O	N	D
ᵗ	29	29	29	28	26	25	24	24	24	25	27	29
☀	8	8	7	7	6	6	6	6	7	7	8	8
💧	17	16	18	17	14	15	16	16	10	8	9	12

Maldives 68

	J	F	M	A	M	J	J	A	S	O	N	D
🌡	29	29	30	31	31	30	29	29	29	29	29	29
☀	9	10	10	8	7	7	7	7	7	7	8	7
💧	3	1	1	3	9	17	14	12	10	11	8	4

Morocco 184

	J	F	M	A	M	J	J	A	S	O	N	D
🌡	18	20	23	26	29	33	38	38	33	28	23	19
☀	7	8	9	10	10	10	9	8	8	8	7	7
💧	5	4	5	3	2	1	0	0	1	4	4	6

New Zealand 154

	J	F	M	A	M	J	J	A	S	O	N	D
🌡	23	24	23	20	17	15	14	15	16	18	20	22
☀	7	7	6	5	5	4	5	5	6	6	6	7
💧	10	9	12	14	16	19	19	19	18	15	13	12

Oman 10

	J	F	M	A	M	J	J	A	S	O	N	D
🌡	20	21	24	28	33	35	37	38	36	32	27	22
☀	8	8	8	10	12	12	10	10	10	10	9	8
💧	1	2	1	2	0	0	0	0	0	0	1	1

Scilly Isles 124

	J	F	M	A	M	J	J	A	S	O	N	D
🌡	9	8	10	12	14	17	19	19	17	15	11	10
☀	2	3	4	6	7	7	7	6	5	3	2	2
💧	22	17	18	15	14	13	12	15	15	18	20	21

Scotland 100

	J	F	M	A	M	J	J	A	S	O	N	D
🌡	5	6	8	11	14	17	18	18	15	12	8	6
☀	1	2	3	5	6	6	5	5	4	3	2	1
💧	21	17	19	16	15	16	16	18	20	20	20	20

South Africa 212

	J	F	M	A	M	J	J	A	S	O	N	D
🌡	33	31	29	25	22	18	19	22	26	28	30	32
☀	10	9	9	9	9	9	9	10	10	10	10	11
💧	8	9	7	3	2	2	2	3	5	7	7	

Spain 112

	J	F	M	A	M	J	J	A	S	O	N	D
🌡	16	17	20	22	27	31	35	35	32	26	20	16
☀	5	6	7	8	10	11	12	11	9	7	5	5
💧	15	13	12	11	8	5	2	3	6	12	12	14

Sri Lanka 62 94

	J	F	M	A	M	J	J	A	S	O	N	D
🌡	28	30	32	32	32	31	31	31	31	30	29	28
☀	7	8	9	8	7	6	6	7	6	6	6	6
💧	5	5	6	11	9	10	8	8	10	15	16	13

Sweden 246

	J	F	M	A	M	J	J	A	S	O	N	D
🌡	-5	-4	1	5	13	17	19	17	12	6	0	-3
☀	1	1	3	5	7	8	7	6	4	2	1	0
💧	16	13	13	11	11	12	15	14	16	15	15	16

Switzerland 240 252

	J	F	M	A	M	J	J	A	S	O	N	D
🌡	-4	-4	-3	0	5	8	11	10	8	5	0	-3
☀	4	5	5	5	5	5	6	6	6	6	4	4
💧	16	15	17	19	19	19	18	19	14	13	13	16

Tanzania 218

	J	F	M	A	M	J	J	A	S	O	N	D
🌡	28	28	28	27	26	25	25	26	28	29	30	29
☀	7	8	7	7	7	8	8	8	8	9	8	7
💧	17	14	17	17	8	2	2	2	1	4	10	18

Thailand 28

	J	F	M	A	M	J	J	A	S	O	N	D
🌡	32	33	34	35	34	33	32	32	32	31	31	31
☀	8	8	8	10	8	7	5	5	5	6	7	8
💧	1	2	3	4	13	14	15	15	17	13	4	1

Turkey 130

	J	F	M	A	M	J	J	A	S	O	N	D
🌡	13	14	16	20	25	29	32	31	28	23	18	14
☀	5	6	7	9	11	13	14	13	11	8	6	5
💧	12	11	9	8	5	4	7	5	6	8	14	

USA: Florida 176

	J	F	M	A	M	J	J	A	S	O	N	D
🌡	21	22	25	28	31	32	33	33	32	29	25	23
☀	7	8	9	9	9	9	9	9	8	7	7	7
💧	8	8	8	5	9	14	16	16	13	8	7	7

USA: Jackson Hole 264

	J	F	M	A	M	J	J	A	S	O	N	D
🌡	-3	0	3	9	15	21	26	25	19	13	3	-2
☀	5	6	8	9	9	11	11	10	9	7	5	4
💧	10	9	11	10	10	8	7	8	7	7	9	10

USA: New York 180

	J	F	M	A	M	J	J	A	S	O	N	D
🌡	-1	1	7	14	21	26	29	27	23	17	10	2
☀	5	6	7	8	9	9	9	8	7	6	4	4
💧	12	11	12	13	12	12	10	11	10	9	13	13

Zambia 226

	J	F	M	A	M	J	J	A	S	O	N	D
🌡	26	27	28	26	25	23	23	26	29	31	30	27
☀	6	6	7	9	9	9	9	10	10	9	8	6
💧	17	16	10	3	0	0	0	0	0	2	8	17

Zanzibar 218

	J	F	M	A	M	J	J	A	S	O	N	D
🌡	28	28	28	27	26	25	25	26	28	29	30	29
☀	7	8	7	7	7	8	8	8	8	9	8	7
💧	17	14	17	17	8	2	2	2	1	4	10	18

CONTRIBUTORS

I couldn't have done it without you – with my heartfelt thanks to…

Pamela Goodman has been a travel writer for eighteen years and is currently the Travel Editor of *House & Garden* and a freelance contributor to a variety of publications including *The Sunday Telegraph* and *How to Spend It*. When not travelling, she divides her time between London and a farmhouse in north Wales, the favourite haunt of her three very spoiled, well-travelled children.

As chief Travel Correspondent for *The Sunday Times* for seventeen years and currently Travel Editor on *Good Housekeeping*, **David Wickers** has travelled to more than a hundred countries in the world, many with his wife and children, two girls now aged eighteen and fifteen and a boy of eight. His expert knowledge on Australia and New Zealand is second to none.

Emma Mahony is currently the Family Travel Editor for The Times Travel Online and lives in London with her three children: Humphrey, nine, and twins Millie and Michael, six. Although travel is her first love, she has worked as Pets, Property, Gardening, Food and Drink, and Shopping Editor during her time at *The Times* as well as writing a column on the joy of twins called Double Trouble.

Annoushka Hempel, fell so in love with Sri Lanka five years ago she decided to move her family there. Now happily installed with sons Otto, eleven, and Milo, eight, who love their exciting lives of jungle, beach and adventure. Her passion for yoga has led to her set up a successful spiritual yoga and wellness retreat in her land of serendipity.

Simon Hills started his career in journalism interviewing pop stars before becoming Associate Editor of *The Times Magazine*. There was a spell running a sailing centre in Greece too, before he settled down in London, with his wife and two daughters. Family holidays are generally taken on the Isle of Wight, but occasionally the parents overcome their pathological dislike of airports to travel further afield.

Safari expert **Charlotte Opperman** has travelled extensively throughout Africa while working for specialist Africa tour operator Aardvark Safaris. She is frequently accompanied by her most demanding clients – her husband and two children.

Amanda Morison is the Travel Editor of *RED* magazine, and has been writing about travel for ten years. Getting on a plane recently got a little more complicated with the arrival of two sons, though both boys are proving expert hotel critics (Feather Down Farm in Hampshire being the current favourite).

Portrait and travel photographer **Hugo Burnand** lives a life balancing his busy London studio with trips to far-flung locations. He was on a four-month backpacking sabbatical around South America with his wife and four children, when he received a call to return to England to photograph the wedding of Prince Charles and Camilla Parker Bowles. His work appears regularly in *Tatler*, and *House & Garden* magazines.

When she's not bombing round the world on a mission, **Lilla Hurst** lives in London with her music producer husband and baby Bertie. She currently works at Channel Five as Head of Co-production following a number of roles in TV production and broadcasting over the past ten years.

Adrian Mourby is a novelist and opera producer but also an inveterate traveller and correspondent for most UK newspapers. He has dragged his teenage children around many of the cultural highlights of this world but found they still prefer Disney.

Say '**Mary Anne Denison-Pender** sent me', to a Maharaja and he'll cry with joy. She has slept in more palaces, met more rajputs, and seen more tigers than you've had onion bhajis. Her long-term love affair with India never wanes – 'I feel unwell unless I get back there every six months,' she says.

CREDITS AND ACKNOWLEDGEMENTS

Once again, my thanks go to all my family, friends and colleagues who have continued to support me with their ongoing enthusiasm and helpful recommendations – and to the hoteliers who welcomed us all. In particular my thanks go to my researcher Amelia Macneal; everyone at Holidays from Heaven; and the ever patient Carole McDonald, Julian Flanders, Daren Booth and Lyn Davies at Butler and Tanner. My most special thanks go to my husband Johnnie and our three fun-loving daughters Rosie, Bella and Francesca without whom *Heaven on Earth Kids* would have been impossible.

None of the hotels in *Heaven on Earth Kids* have paid a fee to be featured. Nor was the author at any stage under any obligation to include them. The final collection has been made from a selection of over 1,000 hotels.

The author would like to thank the following for providing photographs and for permission to reproduce copyright material. While every effort has been made to trace and acknowledge all copyright holders, we would like to apologise should there have been any errors or omissions.

All pictures supplied by the author, contributors, hotels, resorts and tourist boards with special thanks to the following:
Woolley Grange Carole McDonald pages 76–81.
Las Escobas Hugo Burnand pages 148–153.
ICEHOTEL page 250 (*top left*) Photo Big Ben. Artist AnnaSofia Mååg, page 251 Photo Big Ben. Artists Rashid Sagadeev and Leonid Kopeykin.

Please be advised that some of the information contained will have changed since publication. The opinions expressed in this book are those of the author and do not represent the opinions of the publisher. The publisher shall not be liable for any deficiencies in quality, service, health or safety at any of the hotels. All complaints must be made directly to the hotel concerned. While the publisher has made every endeavour to ensure that the information contained in this publication is accurate, it will not be held liable for any expense, damage, loss, disappointment or inconvenience caused, in whole or part by reliance upon such information.

For Rosanna, Isabella and Francesca

First published in 2007
© Sarah Siese and St Christopher's Publishing Ltd

Sarah Siese has asserted her right to be recognised as the author of this work

St Christopher's Publishing Ltd
PO Box 5346, Reading, Berkshire
RG7 2YN

ISBN 978 0 9547 931 3 5 pb
ISBN 978 0 9547 931 2 8 hb

Design, layout, reprographics, printing and binding by Butler and Tanner Limited, Frome and London

Heaven on Earth

A calendar of divine hotels around the world

What they said:

'Every discerning traveller should have a copy on their coffee table'
Sir Richard Branson

'*Heaven on Earth* is an inspired and long overdue collection of the world's best hotels'
Elegant Traveller Magazine

'A must-read offering an inside track for those who truly want to get the very best from their time away'
Kate Thornton, Presenter, *Holiday* BBC1

'Swallow it whole, and take with water'
Ruby Wax

SARAH SIESE